modern publicity

1980

modern publicity

volume 49

1980

Editor Felix Gluck

Studio Vista

ISBN 0 289 70898 2

Printed by Sackville Press Billericay Ltd.

Photoset by Pierson LeVesley Ltd. .

Abbreviations
Abkürzungen

AD Advertiser
Client
Auftraggeber

AG Agency/Studio
Agence/Atelier
Reklameberater

DIR Art director
Directeur artistique
Künstlerischer Leiter

DES Designer/Artist
Maquettiste/Artiste
Grafiker/Künstler

ILL Illustrator/Photographer

Contents

Sommaire

Inhalt

Introduction

This year's dustjacket design is based on a German poster for *Mustang Jeans*. The illustration creates a superbly surrealistic effect and a sense of the toughness both of the model with whom the customer would like to identify and of the material as implied by the razor's edge seat. Jeans and their advertising have been with us for many years now, and it requires style and ingenuity to find new ways and different and surprising angles for their promotion. There are in this issue several other advertisements that focus on jeans, either for their own publicity or to convey an impression of youth or temptation, as in the 'Gold is for Lovers' advertisement on page 72 for instance. I look forward to seeing how jeans are treated in next year's new designs.

It is interesting to find that we have chosen whisky publicity for the openers of both the poster section and the press advertisement section. The ingenuity of ideas and the perfectionism of the presentation make these two campaigns outstanding and I do hope that they are also used outside Great Britain. *White Horse* (pp 16-17) prefers photographic solutions based on visual interpretations of different mixes of whisky, and avoids mentioning the brand name. *Black Label*, on the other hand, uses artwork rather than photography, and proudly displays the label only, without the traditional bottle, although a bottle is shown as part of the image on the stained-glass window advertisement.

In its simplicity and stylish typography, the *Black Magic* advertisement on page 66 also relies on the brand name only.

Albrecht Ade's series of posters (p 27) for the *Landestheater in Darmstadt* succeeds in keeping a uniform housestyle by consistently using a street pavement as a background for the photography.

The poster for the *National Westminster Bank* (p 34) is wittily inspired by the famous *Alka-Seltzer* advertisements, although I doubt whether the promise of quick relief from headaches is fulfilled as successfully as with the real tablets.

In the press advertising section I found the most striking was the promotion of perfume. The advertisements for *Saint Laurent* and *Paco Rabane* on pages 68-69 and that for *Courrèges* on page 73 are beautifully photographed and again show evidence of the tendency away from straightforward illustrations of a product. This applies also to *Guy Bourdin's* superb composition, which remains true to the style with which he made such an impact for *Charles Jourdain* shoes.

In the typeface and bookjacket section I would like to single out *Herb Lubalin's* cover design for 'u&lc' magazine promoting the *American Typeface Corporation* (p 85). Since the appearance of its first issue two years go, under Lubalin's art direction, this magazine has contributed a large variety of ideas and introduced numerous new typefaces in a most pleasing and entertaining way.

In the stamp section we can compare a number of subjects and their solutions. The international year of the child (see p 97) has been celebrated in a variety of ways (see p 97), but the most common has been the easy solution of using children's drawings. The Hungarian post office uses with success the lighthearted child-like drawings by *János Kass*, while the Swedish post office takes a sombre approach by warning us of environmental pollution and showing the child in a gas mask, drawn by *Petter Pettersen*. The commemoration of Einstein's anniversary (p 100) has offered another opportunity for comparison; from the portrayal by *Hans Erni*, which actually appeared several years ago, to the interesting scientific approach in the Mexican stamp by *Gad Almaliah*.

In the letterhead and trademark section the most lively ideas are still those used by designers for their own publicity. With a few exceptions businessmen are still too reticent about their image.

Some of the cosmetics packaging is outstanding for its elegance and luxury, and will surely be kept long after its contents have been used up. For the mass market, the yoghurt packs designed by *Marketing Nord* (p 126) and the designs for *Dymo* tapewriters (p 127) are pleasant in their appeal to children.

In the TV section, the *Rede Globo* designs (pp 143, 149) excel in exploiting the medium to its full extent. Obviously the tradition of kinetic art in Latin America has had its influence here.

In the direct mail section, the integrated material shown by *Smith-Kline French* laboratories on page 174 is very impressive for its appearance and for the effective packaging of tapes and information booklets. *Habitat's* annual review uses an interesting graph in the form of an apple in slices.

The printing ink manufacturers *Gebr. Schmidt* and *Zanders* papers (p 180) exhibit their usual outstanding elegance and lavishness. *Roberto Glussoni's* zodiac symbols for the *Litho-Gamas* calendar (p 186) are beautiful in their simplicity, and *Sam Haskins* had done it again with his highly sophisticated calendar for *Pentax* (p 188).

I would like to thank the contributors, agencies, art directors and clients whose entries have made this issue possible. I hope they will continue to send in their work as before and I also hope that those whose work could not be included in this edition will not be discouraged from entering their work in the future.

Felix Gluck

Introduction

Le sujet de la couverture de l'édition de cette année est basée sur une affiche allemande pour les *Jeans Mustang*. Le résultat est d'un effet surréaliste superbe qui rend magnifiquement l'impression de solidité à la fois du modèle, auquel le client voudrait s'identifier, et du tissu comme veut le montrer le siège en lame de razoir. Nous avons vu depuis plusieurs années déja les jeans et leur publicité et cela demande style et ingéniosité pour trouver des idées nouvelles, différentes et étonnantes pour leur promotion. Il y a dans cette édition d'autres publicités qui se concentrent sur les jeans, soit pour la réclame des pantalons eux-mêmes, soit pour transmettre une impression de jeunesse et de tentation comme par exemple "l'or est pour les amoureux" de la page 2. J'attends avec impatience de voir comment sera traitée la publicité des jeans l'année prochâine.

Il est intéressant de constater que nous avons choisi la publicité pour le whisky comme introduction au chapitre des affiches et de la presse. L'ingéniosité des idées et la perfection de la présentation rendent ces deux campagnes publicitaires exceptionnelles et j'espère qu'elles sont utilisées en dehors de la Grande Bretagne. *White Horse* (pp 16-17) préfère des solutions photographiques basées sur les interprétations visuelles de différents cocktails au whisky et évite de mentionner le nom de la marque.

Black Label au contraire, utilise le dessin plutot que la photographie et exhibe fièrement l'étiquette par elle-même sans la traditionnelle bouteille, bien que l'on montre une bouteille sur le vitrail faisant l'affiche. La réclame de *Black Magic* page 66, s'appuye uniquement sur le nom de sa marque, utilisant la simplicité et l'élégance du caractère d'imprimerie.

La série d'affiches (p 27) *d'Albrecht Ade* pour le *Landestheater à Darmstadt*, réussit à garder un titre uniforme en utilisant comme fond de la photo, les pavés du trottoir. L'affiche de la *Banque National Westminster* (p 34) s'inspire avec esprit de la célèbre réclame *d'Alka-Seltzer*, bien que je doute qu'elle puisse soulager nos maux de tête aussi rapidement que les vrais comprimés.

Parmi les réclames des magazines, celle que je trouve la plus remarquable est la promotion des parfums. Pages 68-69 pour *Saint Laurent* et *Paco Rabane*, page 73 pour *Courrèges*, ces réclames sont de magnifiques photographies et cela montre de nouveau une tendance à s'éloigner de l'illustration directe du sujet. Cela s'applique aussi à la superbe composition de *Guy Bourdin* qui reste fidèle au style qui rendit célèbre les chaussures *Jourdain*.

Dans le chapitre sur les caractères typographiques et de couvertures de livres, je choisirais le dessin de *Herb Lubalin* pour le magazine 'u&lc' lançant l'*American Typeface Corporation* (p 85). Depuis sa parution il y a deux ans, sous la direction artistique de *Lubalin,* ce magazine a contribué à une grande variété d'idées et introduit de nombreux et nouveaux caractères d'une façon des plus agréable et amusante.

Dans le chapitre des timbres nous pouvons comparer un nombre de sujets et leurs solutions. L'année internationale de l'enfant (p 97) a été célébrée de façons bien variées (p 97) mais la plus courante et facile fut d'utiliser des dessins d'enfants. La poste hongroise utilise avec succés les dessins gais et enfantins de *Jànos Kass,* tandis que la poste suédoise prend une vue sombre en nous avisant de la pollution de l'environnement en nous montrant un enfant portant un masque à gaz. La commémoration de l'anniversaire d'Einstein (p 100) offre une autre chance de comparaison: le portrait par *Hans Erni* qui parut il y a quelques années, et l'intéressante approche scientifique du timbre mexicain, par *Gad Almaliah*.

Dans le chapitre des entêtes et marques de maisons les idées les plus intéressantes sont toujours celles utilisées par les dessinateurs pour leur propre publicité. A quelques exceptions près, les hommes d'affaires sont encore trop réservés sur leur image. Certains emballages de cosmétiques sont remarquables par leur luxe et élégance. Ils seront certainement conservés longtemps après que le produit soit épuisé. Pour la production de grande série, les emballages de yaourts de *Marketing Nord* (p 126) et les dessins pour les machines *Dymo* (p 127) sont charmants par leur attraction sur les enfants.

Dans le chapitre sur la télévision, les dessins de *Rede Globe* (p 143 p 149) excellent dans leur exploitation du milieu dans toute son étendue. Il est évident que la tradition de l'art cinétique d'Amerique Latine a laissé son influence içi.

Dans le chapitre sur le brochures, le matériel montré par les laboratoires français de *Smith-Kline-French* page 174 est impressionnant par son apparence et par son emballage éfficace de bandes d'enregistrement et de livrets publicitaires. Le catalogue annuel de Habitat utilise un graphisme intéressant sous forme d'une pomme coupée en tranche.

Les fabricants des encres d'imprimerie *Gebr. Schmidt* et *Zanders* montrent leurs habituelles élégance et prodigalité. Les signes du Zodiaque de *Roberto Glussoni* pour le calendrier *Lithos-Gamas* (p186) sont remarquables par leur simplicité et *Sam Haskins* nous étonne de nouveau avec son calendrier tellement raffiné pour *Pentax* (p 188).

J'aimerais ici remercier collaborateurs, agences, directeurs artistiques et clients dont les envois ont rendu possible cette édition. J'espère qu'ils continueront à nous envoyer leurs oeuvres comme auparavant et j'espère aussi que ceux dont les envois ne furent pas inclus dans ce numéro, ne se décourageront pas d'envoyer leurs oeuvres dans le futur.

Felix Gluck

Einleitung

Unsere Umschlagsillustration für dieses Jahr ist auf ein deutsches Plakat für *Mustang Jeans* basiert. Durch die fast photographische Illustration wurde in diesem Plakat ein bemerkenswerter surrealistischer Effekt erreicht, der gleichzeitig ein Gefühl der Stärke und Zähigkeit übermittelt, mit der sich der Kunde gerne identifiziert. Nebenbei wurde noch durch den Rasierklingensitz die robuste Stärke des Materials betont.

Jeans und deren Reklame sind schon seit Jahren mit uns. Es benötigt Stilgefühl und Erfindungsgabe um neue Wege und interessante überraschende Lösungen für deren Werbung zu finden, denn die Konkurrenz ist gross. In diesem Band haben wir noch verschiedene andere Anzeigen, die auf Jeans eingestellt sind; entweder um Jeans zu verkaufen oder aber um einen Eindruck von Jugend und Versuchung zu erreichen, wie z.B. in dem Inserat *Gold is for Lovers* (S.72). Es wird mich interessieren, zu sehen welche Reklame-Lösungen für Jeans im nächsten Jahr erscheinen werden.

Es ist interessant zu bemerken, dass wir in diesem Band Whisky Reklamen als Öffnungseiten sowohl für den Plakatteil als auch für das Kapitel über Inserate wahlten.

Überraschende Ideen und Perfektion in der Ausführung machten beide Kampagnen besonders bemerkenswert. Ich hoffe dass diese Plakate und Inserate auch ausserhalb England's international verwendet werden.

White Horse Whisky (S 16-17) zeigt die visuelle Erklärung der verschiedenen Weisen Whisky zu trinken durch hervorragende photographische Lösungen, ohne je den Namen des Whisky's zu erwähnen oder eine Flasche zu zeigen. *Black Label* (S 56-57) andererseits verwendet Illustrationen und zeigt stolz nur das Etikett ohne Flasche, obwohl in dem Farbfensterentwurf eine kleine Flasche als Teil des Fensters erscheint. Black Magic Schokoladen (S.66) verwenden auch wiederum nur den Namen in einem stilvoll einfachem Inserat.

Die Plakatserie von Albrecht Ade für das Landestheater in Darmstadt ist konsequent in der Verwendung eines Strassenpflasters als Hintergrund für Photoplakate für ganz diverse Theaterstücke.

Das Plakat für die *Westminster Bank* (S 34) ist eine geistreiche Parodie der bekannten Alka-Seltzer Inserate. Es ist allerdings fragwürdig ob die Bank die Kopfschmerzen so erfolgreich beseitigen kann wie die Tabletten.

Die schönsten Inserate waren die Reklamen für kosmetische Artikel und Parfüms wie z.B. *Saint Laurent* und *Paco Rabane* (S.68-69) und für *Courreges* auf Seite 73. Diese Inserate sind wiederum ein Zeichen der Tendenz, das Produkt in einer mehr subtilen Art und Weise einzuführen. Dies bezieht sich auch auf *Guy Bourdins* immer phantastische Kompositionen wie z.B. dieses Jahr auf Seite 73 in seinem Inserat für *Charles Jourdain* Schuhe.

Im Typographie - und Buchgraphik-Kapitel ist *Herb Lubalin's* Umschlag für 'u&lc' die Zeitschrift der *American Typeface Corporation* besonders eindrucksvoll. Dieses Magazin hat unter *Lubalin's* Leitung seit dem Erscheinen vor zwei Jahren eine Mannigfaltigkeit von amüsanten und interessanten Ideen zur Einführung neuer und auch älterer Buchstaben-typen verwendet.

In dem Briefmarkenentwurfsteil können wir eine Anzahl von thematischen Aufgaben vergleichen.

Das Internationale Jahr des Kindes wurde in grosser Verschiedenheit gefeiert aber die allgemein bequemste Lösung (und vielleicht auch die billigste) war die Verwendung von Kinderzeichnungen. Die ungarische Postverwaltung hat aber zum Beispiel mit Erfolg den Graphiker *János Kass* beauftragt Marken im fröhlichem Stil von Kinderzeichnungen zu entwerfen. Die schwedische Post wiederum warnt uns vor der Gefahr der Umweltverseuchung durch Petter Petterson's Zeichnung eine Kindes in einer Gasmaske. Die Erinnerung an *Albert Einstein's* Geburtstag gibt uns auch Vergleichsmöglichkeiten, von dem ausgezeichneten Portrait von *Hans Erni*, das allerdings schon vor einigen Jahren erschien, bis zu der interessanten teilweise diagrammatischen Lösung für Mexiko von *Gad Almaliah*.

In unserem Kapitel über Schutzmarken und Briefköpfe finde ich, dass die lebhaftesten und interessantesten Ideen noch immer jene sind, die die Graphiker für sich selbst entwerfen. Mit wenigen Ausnahmen sind Geschäftsleute noch immer viel zu zurückhaltend, wenn es sich um das eigene Firmenbild handelt.

Einige der Verpackungsentwürfe sind fast Luxus-objekte die wegen ihrer Eleganz noch jahrelang nach der Verwendung des Inhalts behalten werden.

Für den Mássenmarkt sind die Kinderpäckchen für Jogurt (S.126) und den Dymo-Bandschreiber (S.127) besonders ansprechend.

Im Film und TV-Vorspann Teil sind die Entwürfe für REDE GLOBO (S 143, 149) besonders bemerkenswert, weil sie die Möglichkeiten des Mediums vollkommen ausnutzen. Der südamerkanische Flair für kinetische Kunst ist hier besonders bemerkbar. Im Broschürenteil ist die voll integrierte Kampagne der Smith-Kline Laboratorien mit ihrer koordinierten Verwendung von Kasetten und Broschüren besonders eindrucksvoll.

Habitat verwendet interessante graphische Kurven in der Form von Apfelschnitten für den Jahresbericht der Firma. Die Druckfarbenfabrik Gebrüder Schmidt und auch Zanders Feinpapiere, werben wiederum mit der Eleganz und dem Luxus der Praesentation an die wir schon seit Jahren von diesen Firmen gewöhnt sind. Roberto Glussoni's Tierkreis symbole für den Lithogamas Kalender sind schön in ihrer Einfachkeit, waehrend Sam Haskins uns wiederum mit raffinierten Kalendern Bereichert.

Ich danke allen Graphikern, Werbeagenturen, Hotshops, Firmen und Postdirektionen die mit ihren Einsendungen zur Vielfaltigkeit dieses Buches beigetragen haben. Ich hoffe dass auch jene wiederum teilnehmen werden, deren Arbeiten dieses Jahr nicht erscheinen konnten.

Felix Gluck

Index

Index

Index

Advertisers
Clients
Auftraggeber

1a-d Great Britain
AD White Horse Distillers Ltd
AG French, Cruttenden, Osborn, Ltd
DIR/DES Graeme Norways
PHOTO Nick Hazzard
whisky

1a

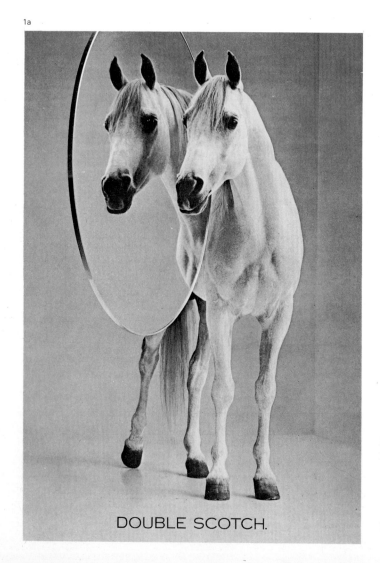

DOUBLE SCOTCH.

1b

SCOTCH AND WATER.

SCOTCH AND GINGER.

1c

1d

NEAT SCOTCH.

Posters
Affiches
Plakate

1 United States
AD Yamaha Motors US
AG Chiat/Day Inc
DIR/DES Lee Clow/Brendon Thomas
PHOTO Lamb & Hall
COPY David Butler
snowmobiles,

2a-b Japan
AD Matsushita Electric Industrial Co Ltd
AG CDP Japan Ltd
DIR/DES (a) Takuya Yamaguchi
(b) David Gribbin
ILL (b) Masami Schimoda, (b) Haruki Hitzuda
COPY David Gribbin
Music Center, Chaine Stereo

3 Great Britain
AD Digital Equipment Corporation
AG Lock/Pettersen Ltd
DIR/DES Tor Pettersen
tailormade computer equipment, équipment
de computer fait sur commande,
spezialangefertigte Computer

4 Germany
AD BASF Aktiengesellschaft
AG BASF/Abtlg Öffentlichkeitsarbeit
DES Franziska Krause
publication

5 United States
AD Koenig Artist Supply
AD Corporate Art Dept
DIR Tony Serino
ILL Joe Morek
COPY Tony Serino
artist's supplies

1

2a

2b

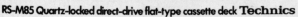

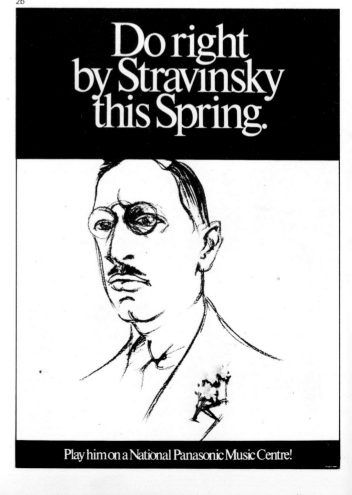

3

4

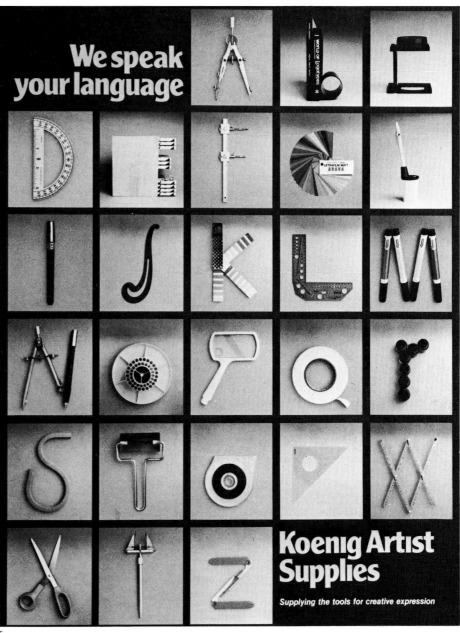

5

Posters
Affiches
Plakate

1 Yugoslavia
AD Mura—Fashion Factory
AG SM Delo
DIR/DES Jani Baučer
ILL Miha Tršar
fashion, mode

2 Japan
AD Kasugai Co Ltd
AG Kasugai Co Ltd
DIR/DES Shozo Murase
ILL Masahiko Fujii
prestige poster

3 Sweden
AD AB Felix
AG Anderson & Lembke AB
DIR/DES Göran Thell
ILL Ronnie Nilsson
COPY Agneta Weiland
photo products, produits à partir de la pomme
de terre, Kartoffel-produkte

4 Great Britain
AD Loveable
DIR S Donoghue
PH A Randall
COPY G Harriss
underwear

5 Israel
AD Sabrina Textile Enterprises
AG Ounaf/Karmon/Shifrin/Na'aman
DIR/DES Yak Milho
ILL Ben Lamm
COPY Tirza Granot
tennis socks, chaussettes de tennis

6 Switzerland
AD Capsugel
AG Dieter Urban
DIR/DES Dieter Urban
ILL Alexander von Steiger
COPY Andreas K Heyne
pharmaceuticals

1

2

3

4

7 Holland
AD Uitgeverij Spaarnestad BV
AG NPO/Nationale Publiciteits Onderneming
BV
DIR/DES Peter Wagner
PHOTO Panorama Magazine
COPY Hugo Nugteren
weekly magazine *Panorama*

8a-b Germany
AD Time Shop Mode
AG Graphik-Desing Akademie der Bildenden
DIR Albrecht Ade
DES/ILL Willi Bunkowski
fashion, mode

5

6

8a

7

8b

1 United States
AD Cornell University
AG/DIR/DES Dru DeSantis
ILL Henry Wolf
call for entries, poster competition,

2 Great Britain
AD Scottish Tourist Board
AG Forth Studios
DIR/DES Andrew Hunter
ILL Jim Gorman
tourism

3 Great Britain
AD Bell's Diner
AG The Small Back Room
DIR/DES/ILL Mark Osborne
restaurant

4a-b Great Britain
AD British Transport Hotels
AG Cato Johnson Ltd
DIR (a) Richard Tilley (b) Leyland Gomez
DES (a) Leyland Gomes, Sue Malin
    (b) Leyland Gomez
ILL (a) Richard Tilley
    (b) Bill Dawson-Thomson
tourism/holidays, tourisme vacances,
Tourismus/Feri

5 Denmark
AD Union of Danish Market Gardeners
AG Weber & Sørensen Reklamebureau A/S
DIR/DES Steen Karup
ILL Poul Ib Henriksen
tulips, Tulpen

2

3

Landscape Architecture Graphics Competition

The First International Competition Of Outstanding Student Work

All students currently enrolled in Landscape Architecture programs are eligible. Work must have been completed during the academic year.

Students may submit an entry for one or more of the following categories:
Plan drawing
Section/elevation drawing
Perspective sketching
Model photography
Functional diagram

Judging will be based on creativity in graphic technique, development of individual style, communication of ideas, professional appearance.

Emphasis is on graphics not technical data.

1st Place, 2nd Place and Honorable Mentions will be awarded in each category. 1st and 2nd Place winners will receive $200.00 and $100.00 respectively. All winners will receive an award certificate and will have their work published.

Entry application forms must be postmarked by December 11, 1978.

All submitted work must be postmarked by February 15, 1979.

For application form and details see department head.

Concours de Dessins D'Architecture Paysagère

Le Premier Concours Des Meilleurs Travaux Estudiantins

Tout étudiant actuellement inscrit dans un programme d'architecture paysagère est éligible. Il faut que le travail ait été accompli pendant l'année scolaire.

Les étudiants peuvent présenter des projets dans une ou plusieurs des catégories suivantes:
Dessin de plans
Dessin de section/élévation
Esquisse de perspectives
Photographie de maquettes
Diagramme fonctionnel

Les projets seront jugés sur la créativité de la technique graphique, le développement du style individuel, la communication des idées et l'apparence professionnelle.

On mettra l'accent sur le dessin, non pas sur les données techniques.

On donnera des prix de premier (1er) et de deuxième (2e) rang, aussi bien que des mentions honorables, dans chaque catégorie. Les gagnants du 1er et 2e rang recevront respectivement des prix de $200 et de $100. Tous les gagnants recevront des certificats, et leurs travaux seront publiés.

Les feuilles d'inscription doivent être timbrées avant le 11 décembre.

Les projets présentés doivent être timbrés avant le 15 février.

S'adresser au chef du département pour les détails et les feuilles d'inscription.

Concurso de Arquitectura Ambiental

La Primera Competencia Internacional De Trabajos Sobresalientes A Ni Vel De Estudiantes.

Todos los estudiantes actualmente matriculados en arquitectura ambiental pueden considerarse como candidatos. El trabajo debe ser terminado durante el año académico.

Los estudiantes se pueden suscribir en una o varias de las siguientes categorias:
Diseño de planos
Diseño seccional y de alzado
Esquema de perspectiva
Fotografía modelada
Diagrama funcional

El juicio se hará en base a la creatividad en la técnica de dibujo, desarrollo del estilo individual, comunicación de ideas y apariencia profesional.

Se hará énfasis en el dibujo, no en datos técnicos.

Serán otorgados primero y segundo puesto además de una mención de honor en cada categoría. Los ganadores del primero y segundo puesto recibirán $200 y $100 dólares respectivamente. Además, todos los ganadores obtendrán un diploma y su trabajo será publicado.

La fecha límite para los formularios de inscripción es el II de diciembre.

La fecha límite para entregar los trabajos es el 15 de febrero.

Para obtener los formularios y más información y detalles, diri girse al Director del departamento.

Landschaftsplanung Graphischer Wettbewerb

Erster Internationaler Wettbewerb Für Hervorragende Studentische Arbeiten.

Teilnahmeberechtigt sind alle gegenwärtig an einem Programm der Landschaftsplanung beteiligten und eingeschriebenen Studenten. Beiträge müssen während des laufenden akademischen Jahres abgeschlossen sein.

Beiträge sollten eine oder mehrere der folgenden Kategorien betreffen:
Planzeichnen
Aufrissquerschnitte
Perspektivische Entwürfe
Modellphotographie
Funktionale Diagramme

Die Bewertung erfolgt nach folgenden Kriterien: Kreativität in der graphischen Gestaltung, Ausbildung des individuellen Stils, Kommunikation von Ideen, Professionelles Erscheinungsbild.

Das Schwergewicht liegt auf graphischer Gestaltung, nicht auf technischen Daten.

Ein erster und zweiter Preis, sowie Ehrenpreise, werden in jeder Kategorie verliehen. Die Gewinner der ersten Preise erhalten je $200, die der zweiten Preise je $100. Alle Gewinner erhalten eine Urkunde; ihre Arbeiten werden veröffentlicht.

Bewerbungen müssen den Poststempel von spätestens 11. Dezember tragen.

Alle vorgelegten Arbeiten müssen bis spätestens 15.Februar bei der Post abgestempelt sein.

Bewerbungsformulare sowie nähere Auskünfte können bei der oben genannten Adresse angefordert werden.

4a

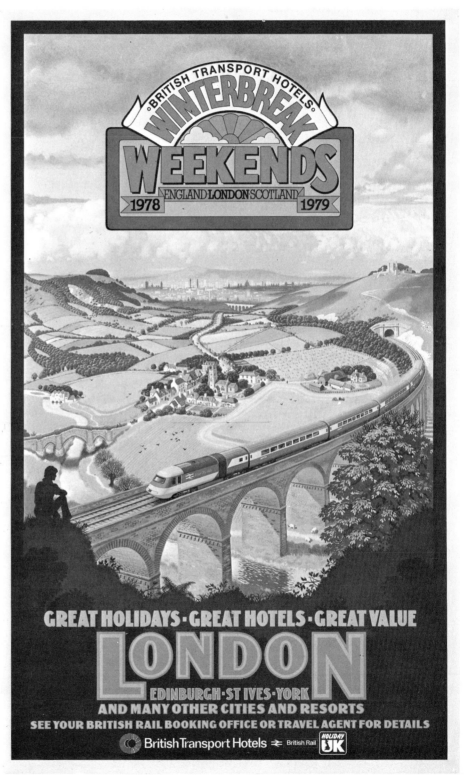

4b

Spring ud og køb tulipaner

5

Posters
Affiches
Plakate

1 United States
AD Goldsholl Associates
AG Goldsholl Associates
DIR/DES Morton Goldsholl
PHOTO Harry Goldsholl
COPY Morton Goldsholl
photo-conversion process, conversion
photographique

2 Germany
AD Solartechnik Berlin
AG Reinhart Braun
DIR/DES Reinhart Braun
ILL H C Suchland
solar energy, Sonnen energieverwendung

3 Great Britain
AD Daily Telegraph
AG Castle Chappell and Partners
DIR John B. Castle
DES Trevor D. Crocker
ILL John Riley
daily newspaper property section, journal
section propriétées, Immobilieninserate einer
Tageszeitung

4 Holland
AD Schaakreade 78
DIR Manfred van de Stolpe
DES Foto & Styling Ton Carstens
non professional chess festival, festival
d'échecs pour amateurs

5 France
AD S.I.C.O.B.
AG Publicis
DIR Jean-Marie Moisan
DES Michel Granger

6 Japan
AD Seibu Department Stores
AG Ikko Tanaka Design Studio
DIR/DES Ikko Tanaka
PHOTO Kishin Shinoyama
the cosmos of Tamasaburoh, l'univers de
Tamasaburoh, die Welt von Tamasaburoh

1

2

Thinking of moving?
The Daily Telegraph
Property Pages

3

5

4

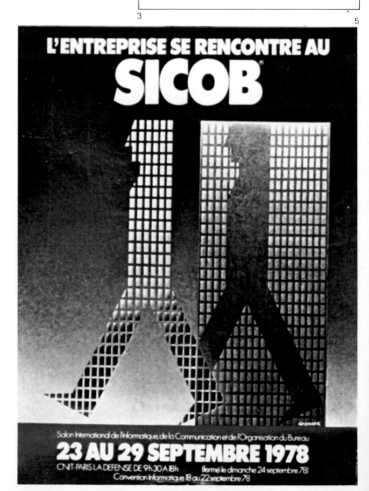

7a/b Great Britain
AD Levis
AG McCanns
DIR Eric Barker
ILL Phil Dobson
Levis Footwear

8a United States
AD Performing Arts Services
AG Fuhrman-Allgood Design
DIR Charles Fuhrman
ILL Edith Allgood
voucher programme for the performing arts

8b-c United States
AD Walnut Creek Civic Arts Association
AG Fuhrman-Allgood Design
DIR/DES Charles Fuhrman
ILL (b) Edith Allgood (c) Charles Fuhrman
   (b) series of lunchtime concerts
   (c) Theatre

6

7a

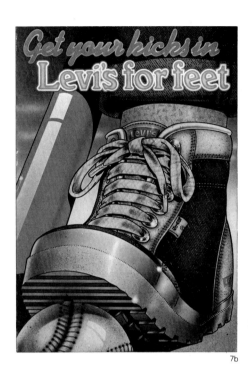

7b

8a

8b

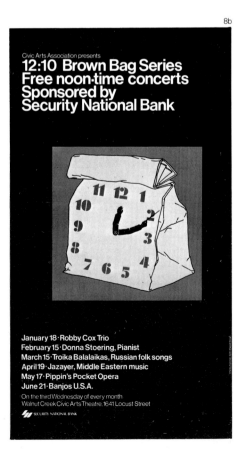

8c

1 Germany
AD Josef Janard
AG Endrikat
DIR/DES Endrikat
ladies' fashions, mode pour dames,
Damenmoden

2a-b Great Britain
AD Mayfair Fashions
AG First City Advertising
DIR Peter Maisey
denim jeans

3 Germany
AD Haus am Waldsee
AG Jürgen Spohn
DIR/DES/ILL Jürgen Spohn
concert

4a-b Germany
AD Landestheater Darmstadt
DIR Albrecht Ade
DES/ILL Richard Muller
Theatre

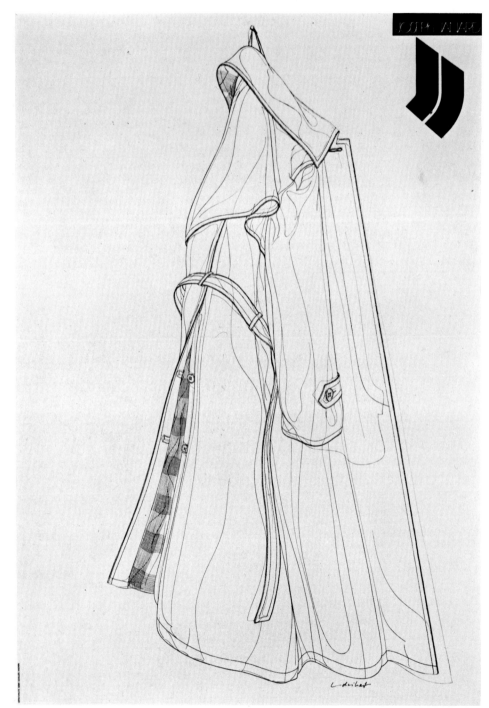

1

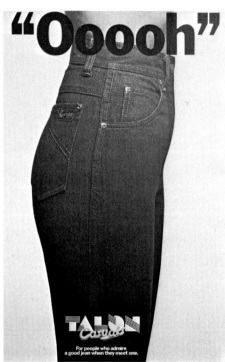

2a

2b

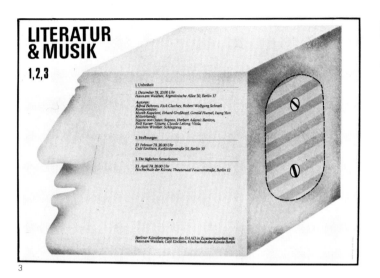

3

4a

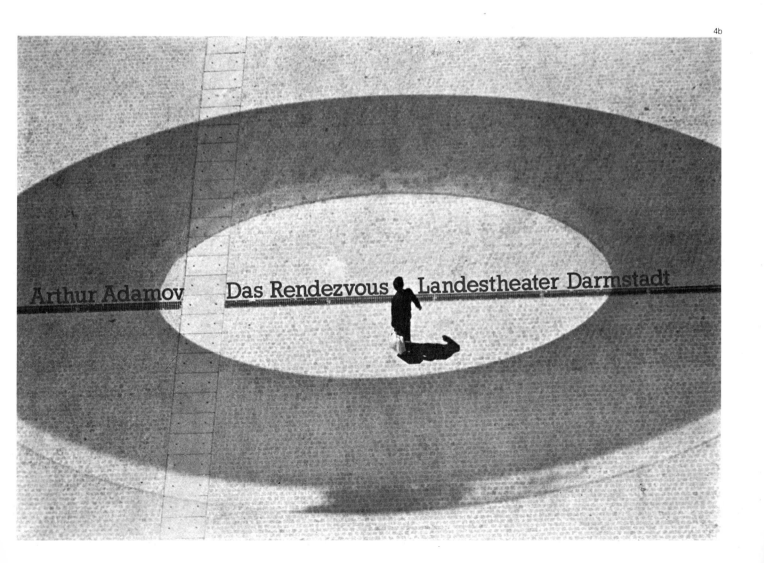

4b

Posters
Affiches
Plakate

1 Great Britain
AD DCA Industries Ltd
AG M.I. Advertising Ltd
DIR N. Belcher
DES P. Fildes
PHOTO John Williams
scones, petits pains, Gebäck

2 Yugoslavia
AD Society of Slovenian Milk Producers
AG SM Delo
DES Jani Bavčer
ILL Milan Pajk
COPY Miro Kline
milk, lait

3 Sweden
AD National Swedish Board for Consumer
Politics
AG Niels Christensen Reklam
DES Niels Christensen
promotion of economy of energy, promotion
pour l'économie de l'énergie,
Energieersparung

4a-b Holland
AD A.S.A.
AG N.P.P.
DIR Eugène van Herpen
DES (a) Dick Splinter (b) Tjend Wynen

5 Brazil
AD Alcantara Machado Comércio e
Empreendimentos Ltda
AG Alcantara Machado, Periscinoto
Comunicaçoes Ltda
DIR/DES Renato Castanhari Jr.
PHOTO Ernest Schauder
COPY Duilio Sarto Filho
International Packaging, Graphic Arts Trade
Fair, foire du emballage et des arts
graphiques, International Verpackungsmesse

2

3

OPERATIE
MOEDERS MOOISTE

Algemene Studenten Arbeidsverlening
Amstelveen, Uilenstede 108 / Amsterdam, Singel 432 / Arnhem, Bakkerstraat 31 / Delft, Koommarkt 82 / Den Haag, Achterom 38 A /
Eindhoven, Kleine Berg 11 / Groningen, Oude Kijk in 't Jatstraat 27 / Leiden, Rapenburg 91 / Rotterdam, Vasteland 29-31 /
Tilburg, Noordstraat 94 / Utrecht, Donkeregaard 2.
Met medewerking van Citroën Nederland.

4a

4b

OPERATIE
GEVULDE EEND

ASA Open huis vindt plaats van 9 tot 18 uur op 28 november in onze kantoren te Eindhoven
(Kleine Berg 11), Groningen (Oude Kijk in 't Jatstraat 27), en Tilburg (Noordstraat 94). Op 29 november in Arnhem (Bakkerstraat 31),
Leiden (Rapenburg 91), Den Haag (Achterom 38A) en Utrecht (Donkere Gaard 2) en op 30 november te Amstelveen (Uilenstede 108),
Amsterdam (Singel 432), Delft (Koommarkt 82) en Rotterdam (Vasteland 29-31). Teams of individuen (dan stellen wij een team samen)
dienen zich zo snel mogelijk in te schrijven op het ASA-kantoor. Operatie Gevulde Eend start steeds om 15 uur om en nabij het ASA-kantoor.
Met medewerking van Citroën Nederland.

5

FIEPAG 79

8ª Feira Internacional de Embalagem, Papel e Artes Gráficas
8th International Packaging, Paper and Graphic Arts Trade Fair
16-25 março/march-Parque Anhembi-São Paulo, Brasil

1a-b India
AD Air-India
AG Air-India Art Studio
DIR J.B. Cowasji
DES S.N. Surti
ILL (a) R.M. Kharat (b) S.A. Gupte
tourism

2 Hong Kong
AD Liu Chong Hing Bank Ltd
AG The Group Advertising Ltd
DIR Kan Tai-keung
DES Kan Tai-keung/Sam Lee Chi-sau
ILL Sam Lee Chi-sau
bank

3 South Africa
AD Safcor (Pty.) Ltd
AG Ian Coetser Associates (Pty.) Ltd
DIR/COPY Ian Coetser
DES Frans Jacobs
shipping, transport

4a-b Japan
AD Yanmar Diesel Engine Co Ltd
AG AN Creative Co Ltd
DIR Tatsundo Hayashi
DES Yukio Akiyama/Junichi Asaka/Mieko
 Ashibe
ILL (a) Kohichi (b) Shoji Takushima
COPY Terence Esmay
 (a) Diesel engine, (b) Generators

5 Argentina
AD Casa de Troya White Wine
AG Lautrec Publicidad
DIR Alfredo Rey
PHO Martin Siccardi
COPY Fernando Pearson
wine

6 Hong Kong
AD Mobil Ltd
AG SS Design & Production
DIR Cheung Shu-Sun/Kan Tai-Keung
DES Kan Tai-Keung/Cheung Shu-Sun
COPY Kan Tai-Keung/Cheung Shu-Sun
gas, oil

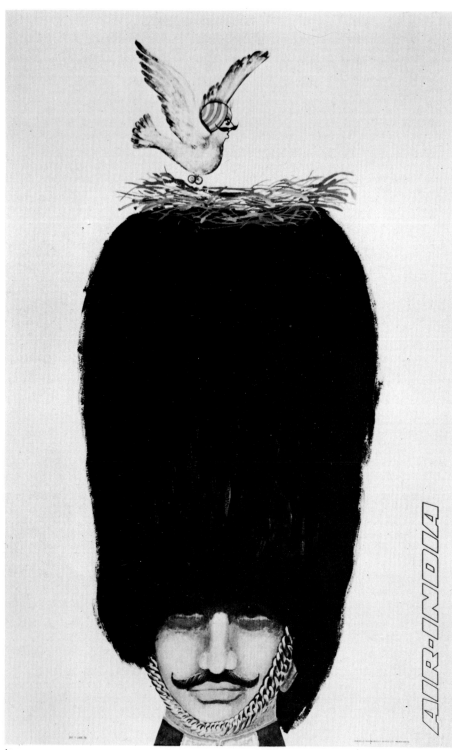

1a

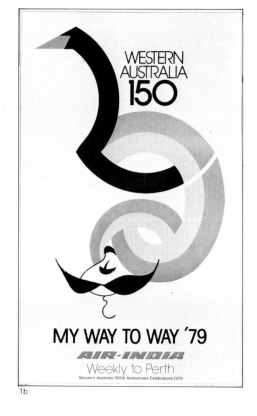

1b

2

3

4a

4b

5

6

1 United States
AD Helene Curtis Ind. Inc.
AG Sinadinos/Gangi Design
DIR/DES Guy Gangi
ILL Gary Taber
COPY Sue Peterson
comb, peigne, kamm

2 Germany
AD Evangelische Kirche Berlin
AG/DIR/DES Reinhart Braun
ILL Harry C. Suchland
public evangelistic meeting, réunion
évangéliste publique

3 Japan
AD Sangetsu Co Ltd
DIR/DES Shunichi Nakashima
department store, magasin, Warenhaus

4 Italy
AD C. Olivetti & C. SpA
AG Ufficio Pubblicità Olivetti
DIR/DES Franco Bassi
office equipment

5 Australia
AD Australian National University
AG ANV Graphic Design
DIR/DES Adrian Young
lecture by Australian writer

6 Italy
AD (a) Mocauto (b) Fiat
AG Ethos
DIR Angelo Colella
DES (a) G. Carloni (b) F. Falcioni
COPY Alberto Vitali
motor cars

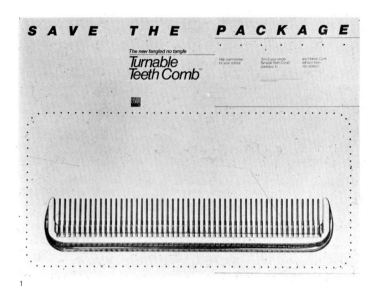

1

2

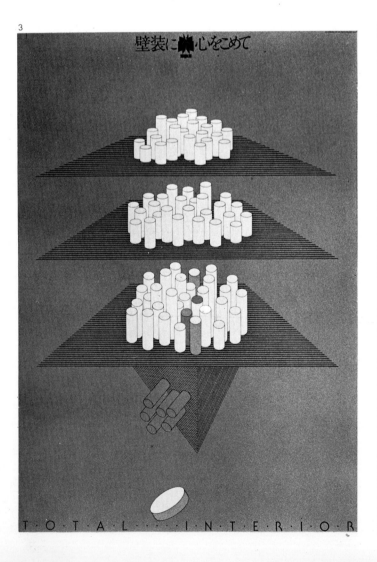

3

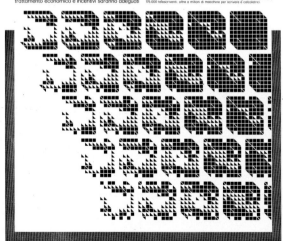

4

7 Belgium
AD Theatre de Poche, Bruxelles
DES Jacques Richez
theatre

8 Italy
AD Ente Provingiale Per il Turismo
AG Studio de Santis
DIR Alfredo de Santis
DES Alfredo de Santis
flower carnival, festival des fleurs,
Blumenfest

32-33

5

6a

6b

8

7

Posters
Affiches
Plakate

1 Great Britain
AD National Westminster Bank
AG J. Walter Thompson
DIR Mike Preston
DES Mike Preston/Ian Hutton
PHOTO Michael English
COPY Ian Hutton
bank

2 Spain
AD Salon Nautico de Barcelona
AG/DIR/DES Enric Huguet
boatfair

3 Germany
AD Film Festspiele Berlin
AG Atelier Noth & Hauer
DES Volkes Noth, Cordes Hauer, Peter
Sodemann, Gloria Reinke
ILL Noth, Hauer, Sodemann, Klappert
film festival

4a-b Italy
AD Assessorato alla Cultura del Commune de
Roma
AG Guiliano Vittori
DIR/DES Guiliano Vittori
film festival

5 Germany
AD Georg Dommel
AG Werbestudio Hippler
DIR/DES Eberhard Hippler
COPY George Dommel
drive-in cinema

6 France
AD Centre Georges Pompidou
AG Roman Cieslewicz
DIR Pontus Hullten
DES Roman Cieslewicz
Paris-Berlin Exhibition 1900-1930

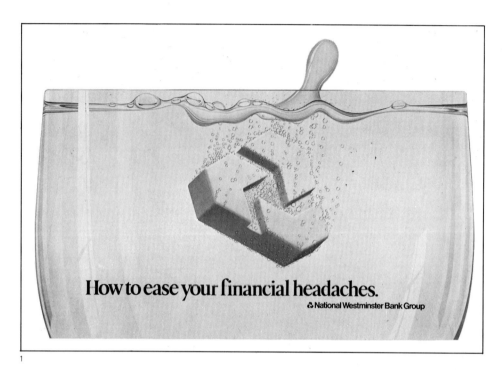

1

2

3

4a

7 Spain
AD E.M.A.V.
AG José Ros Gonzàlez
DIR/DES/COPY José Ros Gonzàlez
Exhibition

8 United States
AD Massachusetts Institute of Technology
AG MIT Design Services
DES Jacqueline S. Casey
Exhibition

4b

5

6

7

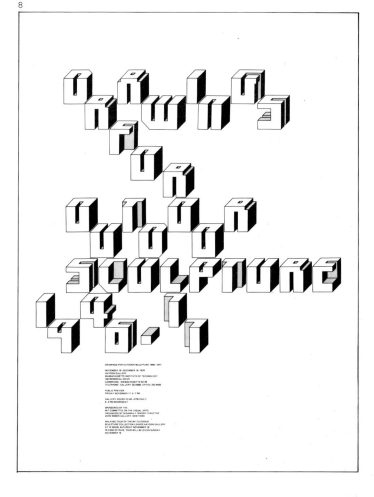

8

Posters
Affiches
Plakate

1a-b-c Italy
AD La Rinascente
AG La Rinascente Ufficio Pubblicità
DIR/DES Ettore Mariani
PHOTO (a) Gianni Ghezzi, (b) Tino Crippa,
(c) Nino Mascardi
(a) furniture fabrics, garnitures de mobilier,
Möbelstoffe, (b) bathroom ideas, idées pour
salle de bain, (c) fashions, modes

2a-b Great Britain
AD Home Office
AG Central Office of Information
DIR Alan Gatland
DES/ILL Banks and Miles
anti-theft campaign, campagne anti-vol,
Warnung vor Diebstählen

3 United States
AD GTR Wallcovering Co/Lionel Libson
AG/DES Alan Wood Graphic Design
ILLUS: Cal Sacks
PHOTO: Vince Lisanti
wallpapers

4 Brasil
AD Mercedes Benz do Brasil
AG Standard Ogilvy & Mather
DIR Pierre Affonso Rousselet
DES Jose Carmo da Silva
spare parts for cars

1a

1b

muoversi al sole

/R

1c

WHO'S CALLING AT YOUR HOME?

An open window, an unlocked door...
classic invitations to the burglar.
But so are windows which
are only closed with a simple latch.
Be secure; fit good quality locks
on doors *and windows!*

Watch out...

2a

WHO'S RIDING YOUR BIKE?

Bicycles are an easy target
for thieves – they're easy to take,
and easy to get rid of.
Keep a note of the make, model
and frame number, and...
If you leave it *use a padlock.*

Watch out...

2b

3

Scrubbable-Strippable

ARTISTRY

Richly textured wall covering coordinates

Fashion Vinyl Wall Fabric

4

Não jogue no escuro.
Use sempre peças genuínas.

Mercedes-Benz

Posters
Affiches
Plakate

1 United States
AD Smith Kline and French Labs.
AG Smith Kline and French Labs.
DIR J. Robert Parker
DES Ford-Byrne
ILL Bill Farrell
COPY Carver Portlock
urban immunization, Immunisations
Kampagne

2 Australia
AD ANU Convocation
AG ANU Graphic Design
DIR/DES/ILL Mary-Jane Taylor
luncheon lecture on Aboriginal Rights,
conférence dur les droits des Aborigenes,
Rechte der Eingeborenen

3 Czechoslovakia
AD Exposition 'Ostrava '78'
AG Dilo
DIR Ing Jaroslav Kocur
DES/ILL/COPY Stanislav Kovář
exhibition on environment, exposition sur
l'environement

4a-b United States
AD Container Corporation of America
DIR/DES Jeff Barnes
(a) copy Jeff Barnes/Sharon Woods,
(b) Amy Bacon
(a) crusade of mercy charity organisation, une
croisade de charité, (b) Exhibition

5 Japan
AD La Pola Nara Co Ltd
AG Toguchi Art Studio
DES Tsutomu Toguchi
children's art contest, concours artistique
pour enfants, Ausstellung von Kinderkunst

6 Great Britain
AD North Staffordshire Polytechnic
AG/DIR/DES Graham Stevens
exhibition of the work of Hans Schleger,
exposition de l'oeuvre de Hans Schleger

1

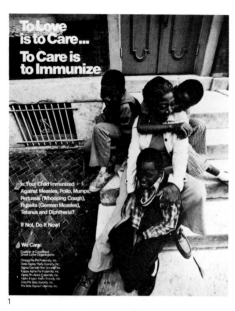

2

3

4a

4b

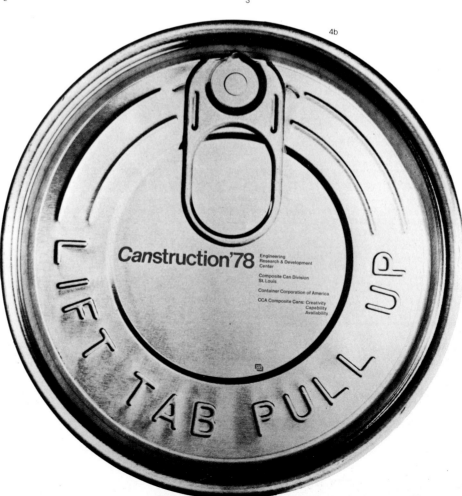

7 Bulgaria
AD Union of Bulgarian Artists
DIR Georoge Petrov
DES Jordan Petrov
exhibition B. Efimov, exposition B. Efimov

8a-b Germany
AD Horst und Irene Follman
DES/ILL Herbert Wenn
two-sided poster for a wedding celebration,
affiche pour célébration de mariage

5

6

7

8a

8b

**Posters
Affiches
Plakate**

1 Germany
AD/AG Stadtverwaltung Erlangen
DES/ILL Walter Tafelmaier
tourism

2 United States
AD Massachusetts Institute of Technology
AG MIT Design Services
DES Jacqueline S. Casey
lectures

3 Great Britain
AD Nature Conservancy Council
AG Conran Associates
DIR Robert Budwig
ILL Terence Lambert
wildlife protection

4a-c Germany
AD Staatliches Naturhistorisches Museum
Braunschweig
AG Hochschule für Bildande Künste,
Braunschweig
DIR Klaus Grözinger
DES Angelika Otte
museum poster, affiche de musée

5 Japan
AD Gallery Takega
AG Media Co Ltd
DIR Shigeo Okamoto
DES/ILL Masakazu Tanabe
decorative poster, affiche décorative

1

2

3

4a

5

4b

4c

**Posters
Affiches
Plakate**

1 Germany
AD Noth & Hauer
AG Atelier Noth & Hauer
DES Volker Noth/Cordes Hauer/Peter
Sodemann
PHOTO Hartwig Klappert
Chirstmas poster, affiche pour Noël,
Weihnachtsplakat

2a-b France
AG Roman Cieslewicz
DIR/DES Roman Cieslewicz
exhibitions

3a-b Germany
AD (a) Theaterhaus Offenburg
   (b) Kammer theater Köln
DIR Albrecht Ade
DES/ILL Claude Shade
theatre

4 Brazil
AD Fred Jordan Communicaçao Visual
DIR/DES Fred Jordan
exhibition of graphic artist's works,
exposition de l'oeuvre graphique de l'artiste

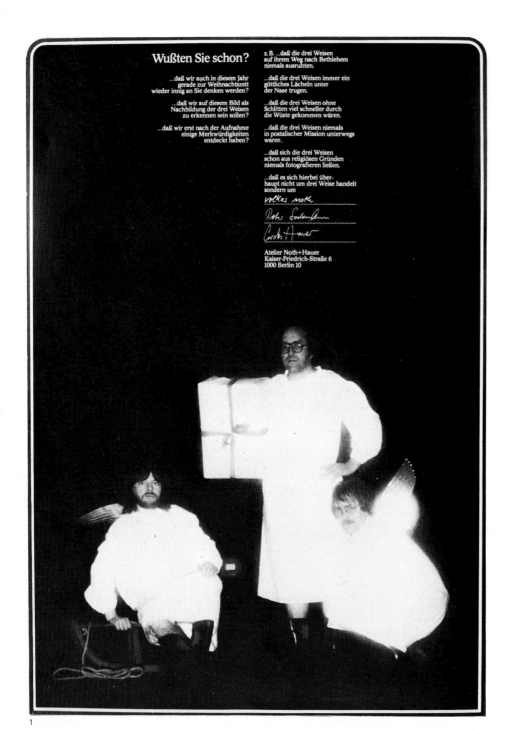

1

2a

2b

3a

3b

4

1 Hungary
AG Offset Nyomda
DIR Lénárt Istvánné
DES István Orosz
international children's day, journée
internationale de l'enfant

2 United States
AD Contemporary Arts Center
AG Lipson-Jacob Assoc.
DIR/DES Stan Brod
COPY Ruth Meyer
exhibition

3 Israel
AD Hassneh Insurance Co
AG Dahaf
DIR I. Koren
ILL Paul Kor
Insurance

4 United States
AD Massachusetts Institute of Technology
AG MIT Design Services
DES Ralph Coburn
lectures

5 Hungary
AD Mokép
AG Mahir
DES/ILL Bakos István
film

6 Great Britain
AD Royal Shakespeare Company
AG CS and S Design Partnership
DIR Malcolm Swatridge
DES Richard Ward
theatre

1

2

3

7 Germany
AD Evangelischer Bund, Bensheim
AG Reinhart Braun
DIR/DES Reinhart Braun
ILL Harry C. Suchland
public lecture

8 Germany
AD Progress Film-Verleih
DIR Otto Kummert
DES Thomas Schallnau
film

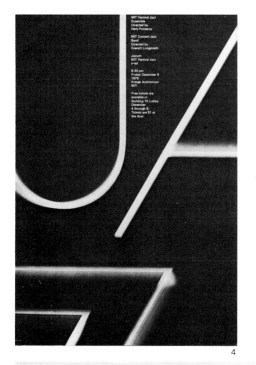

4

5

6

7

8

Posters
Affiches
Plakate

1 Germany (DDR)
AD Universität Rostock
DES Feliks Büttner
club

2 Israel
AD Defence Ministry
DES/ILL Cyla Menusy
appeal for new ideas for efficiency
appel pour de nouvelles idées sur le
rendement, Aufruf für neue Ideen zur
Rationalisierung

3 Germany
AD Deutsche Film und Fernsehakademie
AG Reflex
DIR/DES/COPY Ludvik Feller
film

4 United States
AD Penn State Continuing Education
AG Lanny Sommese Design
DIR/DES/ILL Lanny Sommese
ceramic conference, conférence sur la
céramique

5 Bulgaria
AD Satiric Theatre, Sofia
DES Ludmil Chehlarov
theatre

6 Bulgaria
AD Bulgarian Artist Union
DES/COPY Vemi Kantardjieva
exhibition

7 Finland
AD Kuopion Kaupunginteatteri
AG/DIR/DES Kari Piippo
theatre

1

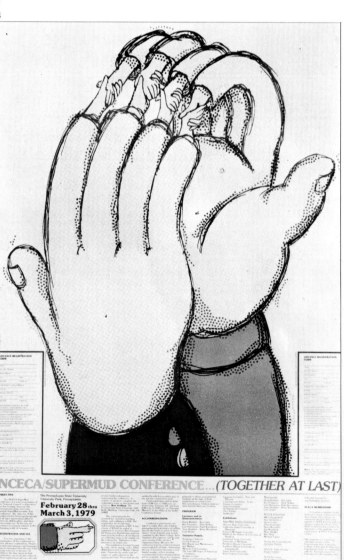

2

4

3

5

6

7

Posters
Affiches
Plakate

1a Australia
AD Student Organisation, Australian National
University
AG ANU Graphic Design
DIR/DES/ILL Adrian Young
children's holiday activities, activités de
vacances pour enfants, Ferienbeschäfrigung
für kinder

1b Australia
AD Australian Bi-Centenary History Project
AG ANU Graphic Design
DIR/DES Adrian Young
conference on Australian history
conférence sur l'histoire de l'Australie,
Konferenz uber Australische Geschichte

2 Spain
AD Salon Nautico
DIR/DES/ILL Bartolome Liarte
exhibition

3 Germany
AD Fachhochschule für Verwaltung, Berlin
AG Reinhart Braun
DIR/DES Reinhart Braun
ILL Harry C. Suchland
public lectures, conférences publiques

4 Spain
AD Salón de la Infancia y la Juventud
AG F. Bas
DIR/DES Francisco Bas
children's exhibition, exposition des enfants

5 Germany
AD Europa Union Berlin
AG Atelier Noth & Hauer
DES Volker Noth, Cordes Hauer, Peter
Sodemann
PHOTO/COPY Noth & Hauer
Europa Day

1a

2

1b

3

4

6 France
AD Ville du Havre
AG Grapus
DIR/DES Collectif Grapus
14th July celebrations, Franz. National feirtag

7 Italy
AD Olivetti SpA
AG Ufficio Pubblicità Olivetti
DIR/DES Franco Bassi
office machines

8 United States
AD Smithsonian Traveling Exhibit Service
AG Bill Caldwell Graphics
DIR/DES Bill Caldwell
PHOTO Joe Goulait
ILL Juan Calderon
COPY Andrea Stevens
travelling exhibition of Latin American
Artistes, exposition ambulante d'artistes
d'Amérique Latine

5

6

8

7

1 Germany (DDR)
AD Progress Film-Verleih
DIR Otto Kummert
DES Marlies Schlegel
film

2 Hungary
AD Szolnoki Sainhàz
DIR István Pál
DES István Orosz
theatre

3 Yugoslavia
AD Studio of Contemporary Dance, Zagreb
AG Zeljko Borčić
DIR/DES Zeljko Borčić
ILL Fedja Fatičić
contemporary dance group, groupe de dance
contemporaine, modernes Ballet

4 Finland
AD Kuopion Kaupunginteatteri
AG Kari Piippo
DIR Kari Piippo
theatre

5 Israel
AD The Jerusalem Khan Theatre
AG Studio Rafi Etgar
DES Rafi Etgar
theatre

6 Italy
AD Cooperative Teatrale Majakovskij
DES Giovanni Luzzi/Paolo Trucco
Theatre

7 Great Britain
AD Kilkenny Arts Week
AG Kilkenny Design Workshops
DIR/DES/ILL Richard Eckersley
arts festival

5

6

7

**Posters
Affiches
Plakate**

1 Japan
AD Shoji Yoshida
AG Kasugai Co Ltd
DIR/DES/COPY Shozo Murase
PHOTO Shoji Yoshida
photographic exhibition

2 Italy
AD Arflex
AG Studio Vitale
DIR/DES Ettore Vitale
exhibition of interior design

3 Poland
AD Polish Jazz Sciety
DES/COPY J. Rafal Olbinski
jazz festival

4 Japan
AD Bologna Book Fair
DES Yutaka Sugita
Bologna Book Fair Year of the Child poster

5 Germany
AD BASF Aktiengesellschaft
AG BASF Aktiengesellschaft Grafisches Büro
DIR/DES Ulrich Höfs
plastics

6 Germany
AD Firma Bauer Getriebe-Motoren
DIR Albrecht Ade
DES Regina Diedenhofen
exhibition

1

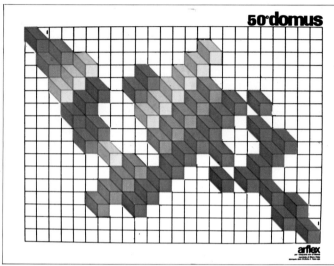

2

3

4

7 Germany
AD Goethe-Institut
AG Horstmann & Werbung
DIR/DES Uwe M. Horstmann
ILL Harald Kull
poster exhibition, exposition d'affiches

8 Japan
DIR Shunichi Nakashima
DES Syunyo Yamauchi
department store

9 Japan
AD Seibu Theater
AG Ikko Tanaka Design Studio
DIR/DES Ikko Tanaka
ILL Haruo Takino
theatre

5

6

7

8

9

Posters
Affiches
Plakate

1 Germany
AD Tanztheater Wuppertal
AG/DES Presse und Werbeamt
Theatre

2 Brazil
AD Camara Brasileira do Livro
AG/DES Santos & Santos
book exhibition

3 Germany
Ad Hochschule für Gestaltung, Offenbach
DIR/DES Helmut Kraft
ILL Uschi Plath
PHOTO Helmut Kraft
Exhibition

4 Germany
AD Progress Film-Verleih
DIR Otto Kummert
DES Heinke, Holm
film

5 Japan
AD Nippon Design Gakuin
AG Media Co Ltd
DIR/DES Masakazu Tanabe
PHOTO Toshiuyki Ohashi
COPY Ken Nishio
Festival of Design School, Festival d'une
école de dessin

TANZTHEATER WUPPERTAL

renate wandert aus

OPERETTE VON PINA BAUSCH

1

2

Na V Bienal do Livro o grande premiado é você.

Vá e ganhe carros, viagens, motos e muitos outros prêmios

V BIL · Pavilhão da Bienal · Ibirapuera
de 11 a 20 de Agosto

PROMOÇÃO: Câmara Brasileira do Livro · Fundação Bienal de São Paulo · Instituto Nacional do Livro.   PATROCÍNIO: Secretaria de Cultura, Ciência e Tecnologia do Estado de São Paulo · Secretaria Municipal de Cultura de São Paulo.

Ausstellung im Stadttheater

Hochschule für Gestaltung
Offenbach am Main

Fachbereich:
Visuelle Kommunikation

Stadttheater Remscheid
vom 19.3. bis 26.4.1978
geöffnet:
mittwochs und samstags
sonntags von 15 bis 18 Uhr
sonntags von 11 bis 13 Uhr
und zu allen Veranstaltungen

Eröffnung:
Sonntag, 19.3.1978
um 11.15 Uhr

3

Alain Delon und Jeanne Moreau in

Monsieur

KLEIN

Ein französisch-italienischer Farbfilm

REGIE: Joseph Losey

4

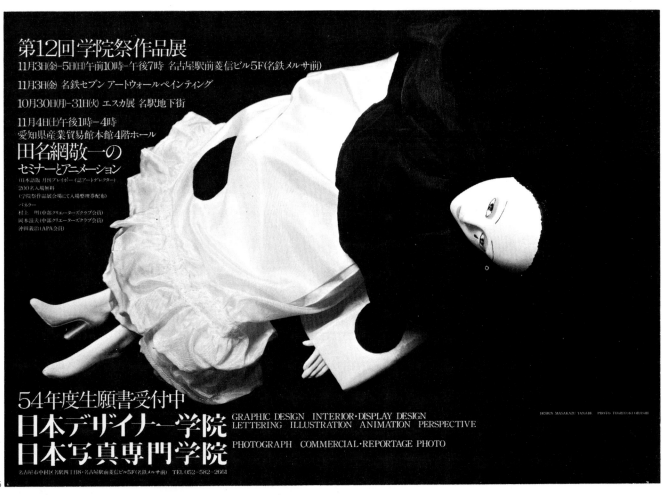

第12回学院祭作品展
11月3日(金)～5日(日)午前10時～午後7時 名古屋駅前菱信ビル5F(名鉄メルサ前)

11月3日(金) 名鉄セブン アートウォールペインティング

10月30日(月)～31日(火) エスカ展 名駅地下街

11月4日(土)午後1時～4時
愛知県産業貿易館本館4階ホール
田名網敬一の
セミナーとアニメーション
(日本語版 月刊プレイボーイ誌アートディレクター)
200名入場無料
(学院祭作品展会場にて入場整理券配布)
パネラー
村上 明(中部クリエーターズクラブ会員)
岡本温夫(中部クリエーターズクラブ会員)
沖田義治(APA会員)

DESIGN: MASAKAZU TANABE   PHOTO: TOSHIYUKI OHASHI

54年度生願書受付中
日本デザイナー学院
日本写真専門学院

GRAPHIC DESIGN   INTERIOR·DISPLAY DESIGN
LETTERING   ILLUSTRATION   ANIMATION   PERSPECTIVE
PHOTOGRAPH   COMMERCIAL·REPORTAGE PHOTO

名古屋市中村区名駅四丁目8·名古屋駅前菱信ビル5F(名鉄メルサ前)   TEL 052-582-2661

5

Press advertisements
Annonces de presse
Zeitungs-Inserate

1a-d Great Britain
AD John Walker & Sons
AG TBWA
DIR Charlotte Sherwood
ILL (a) Nicola Bayley, (b) In-house-studio,
    (c) Larry Learmonth, (d) Malcolm Fowler
COPY Lyndon Mallet

1a

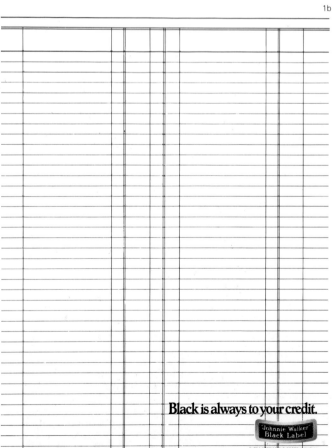

1b

1c

A · LITTLE · BLACK · LOOKS · BEAUTIFUL · IN · GLASS

"Johnnie Walker"
Black Label

EXTRA · SPECIAL · OLD · SCOTCH · WHISKY

Press advertisements
Annonces de presse
Zeitungs-Inserate

1a-b Denmark
AD Tandberg Radio
AG Young & Rubicam
DIR Søren Parup
ILL Piotr
COPY Hans Djurhuus
colour T.V.

2 Great Britain
AD B.H. Morris & Co. (Radio)
AG Abbott Mead Vickers/SMS
DIR/DES Ron Brown
ILL Julian Cottrell
COPY Malcolm Gluck
the Trio Quartz turntable, tourne-disque du
Trio Quartz

3 Great Britain
AD Health Education Council
AG Saatchi & Saatchi Garland-Compton Ltd
DIR Alan Midgley
COPY James Cowther
anti-alcoholism

4 Britain
AD Parker Pens
AG Collet, Dickenson, Pearce & Ptnrs.
DIR Robert Morris
PHOTO Graham Ford
COPY Alfredo Marcantonio
pens

5 Italy
AD Pentel
AG Ethos
DIR Angelo Colella
DES M. Fuzellier
COPY Alberto Vitali
ballpoint pens

6 Great Britain
AD Bulova U.K. Ltd
AG Newton & Godin Ltd
DIR Reg Godin
DES Colin Shoard
ILL Derek Seaward
COPY Reg Godin
watches, montres, Uhren

En Tandberg gi'r sig ikke ud for mere end den er.

TD 20 Actilinear. En oplevelsesmaskine fra Tandberg. Selv i morgen en af verdens mest avancerede båndoptagere. Actilinear er et nyt revolutionerende patentbeskyttet indspillesystem - opfundet af Tandberg som erstatning for det velkendte Crossfield system. Det giver en forbedring i signalbehandlingen på hele 20 DB. Det betyder et radikalt bedre signal/støjforhold end hidtil eksisterende indspillesystemer. Tandberg 20 A er totalt elektronisk styret - og som ekstra udstyr findes en trådløs, infrarød fjernbetjeningsenhed.

Selvfølgelig er der en naturlig sammenhæng mellem din musikmaskine og den lyd, du vil have. Og Tandberg står gerne bag en stor musikoplevelse. Uden at forstyrre det væsentlige - lyden.
Så hvis du alligevel vil ofre en mindre formue på en stor musikoplevelse, kan du lige så godt høre på en Tandberg først som sidst.
Gå ind hos din radioforhandler og få en brochure om TD 20 A med det revolutionerende nye indspillesystem.

TANDBERG
Før eller siden ender du alligevel
med Tandberg.

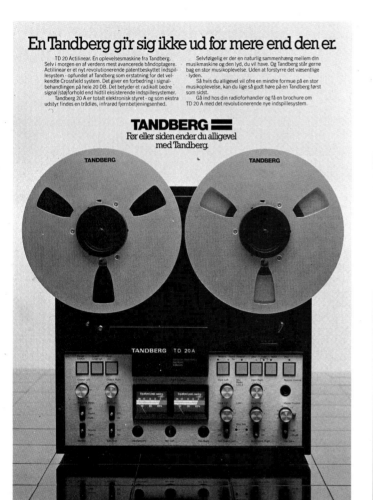

1a

Der er mange måder at se farve-TV på, selv om solen skinner.

Måske er den med papkassen at gå til yderligheder. Man kan selvfølgelig også bare køre fjernsynet ind i et klædeskab. Eller vente til det bliver overskyet...
Men den nemmeste måde er Tandberg.
Alle Tandberg farve-TV har nemlig High-Bright billed-rør. Det betyder, at lysstyrken er øget med ca. 70% i forhold til almindelige farve-TV - og så spiller selv det kraftigste solskin ingen rolle. Billedet står skarpt med helt klare farver og naturtro billeder.
Men lyden er jo næsten lige så vigtig som billedet. Derfor har Tandbergs farve-TV både bas- og diskantkontroller - endda af Baxendall typen, der normalt kun findes i avanceret Hi-Fi udstyr. Tandberg har gjort meget ud af at få farve-TV til at fungere som smukke møbler. Med et tidløst design i ædle træsorter glider et Tandberg farve-TV naturligt ind i ethvert hjem.

Der findes fjernbetjenings-modeller i både 26" og 22". Fjernbetjeningsenheden arbejder med funktionssikkert infrarødt lys - og er forsynet med lige så letgående taster som selve apparatet.
Og så har Tandberg farve-TV markedets laveste effektforbrug (max. 110 W). Det betyder meget for holdbarhed og driftsikkerhed.

CTV 172 22", teak (med fjernbetjening). Kr. 7.285,-
+ merpris for palisander.
CTV 173 26", teak
(med fjernbetjening). Kr. 8.010,-
+ merpris for palisander.
CTV 162 22", teak. Kr. 6.875,-
+ merpris for palisander.
CTV 163 26", teak. Kr. 7.490,-
+ merpris for palisander.
CTV 164 26", palisander med
jalousi. Kr. 8.520,-

TANDBERG
værd at se på
- også langt frem i tiden.

1b

2
3

The base of real wealth.

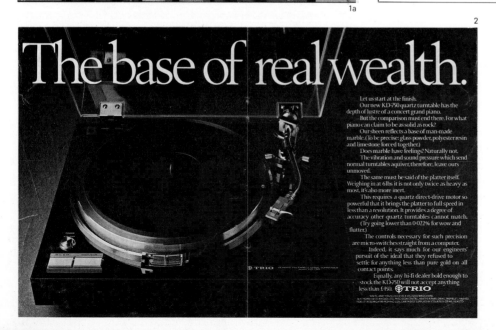

Let us start at the finish.
Our new KD-750 quartz turntable has the depth of lustre of a concert grand piano.
But the comparison must end there. For what piano can claim to be as solid as rock?
Our sheen reflects a base of man-made marble. (To be precise: glass powder, polyester resin and limestone forced together.)
Does marble have feelings? Naturally not.
The vibration and sound pressure which send normal turntables aquiver, therefore, leave ours unmoved.
The same must be said of the platter itself. Weighing in at 6lbs it's not only twice as heavy as most, it's also more inert.
This requires a quartz direct-drive motor so powerful that it brings the platter to full speed in less than a revolution. It provides a degree of accuracy other quartz turntables cannot match.
(Try going lower than 0.022% for wow and flutter.)
The controls necessary for such precision are micro-switches straight from a computer.
Indeed, it says much for our engineers' pursuit of the ideal that they refused to settle for anything less than pure gold on all contact points.
Equally, any hi-fi dealer bold enough to stock the KD-750 will not accept anything less than £450. **TRIO**

If you drink too much there's one part that every beer can reach.

Your health isn't the only thing which suffers if you over-drink. A night of heavy drinking can make it impossible for you to make love.
And even if you think your drinking isn't affecting you, have you ever wondered how it might be affecting your partner?
Put it this way. How would you like to be made love to by a drunk?
The Health Education Council. Everybody likes a drink. Nobody likes a drunk.

7 Brazil
AD Embraer-Emp. Brasileira de Aeronáutica
AG DPZ Propaganda
DIR Francisco Petit
ILL Abraham Lincoln
COPY Washington Olivetto
aeroplanes

8 Sweden
AD Electrolux constructor
AG Anderson & Lembke Vintergatan AB
DIR Frank Gabriele
cleaners

9 Great Britain
AD Olivetti
AG Cherry Hedger & Seymour
DIR/DES T. Muranka
ILL Bruce Brown
COPY G.B. Seymour
calculators, machines à calculer

58-59

It takes 15 operations to form the nib. Parts are manufactured to 1/1,000 of an inch. 28 hours are spent polishing the trim. Every pen is written with, cleaned then inspected.

At the foot of the page is a new Parker pen, the Falcon.
It is unlike any other pen.
It does not have a separate nib.
Instead, we beat the nib from the stainless steel casing.
Although the Falcon is a new design, in many ways it is precisely the same as our other pens.
We coat the arrow clip and the barrel band with a layer of gold. Then we polish them in a slowly revolving barrel full of walnut chippings.

Today, when a car is turned out in hours we still take six days to make a pen.

We tip each nib with Plathenium. An alloy four times stronger than steel.
And we split the nib as we have always done; by hand, using a microscope and a blade no thicker than a human hair.
To build a pen in this way takes money as well as time.
The Parker Falcon will cost you as much as £15·00. A lot to pay for a pen. Very little for a week's work.

✦PARKER

4

Le Pentel verdi spuntan come funghi.

Ball Pentel
Pentel verde. Dal Giappone.

5

Bulova is about to enter a completely new and exciting phase in the company's history. For years the name Bulova has been synonymous throughout the world with high quality products. Now with new management and a new product range Bulova are poised for a breakthrough into the mid to high price market. This autumn sees the biggest ever advertising campaign yet staged for the Bulova brand. Double page spreads in full colour dramatically expose Bulova's new image of quality and style. Advertising will be appearing in the Sunday Times Magazine, Observer Colour Magazine and Telegraph Sunday Magazine from the beginning of September through to Christmas. This distinctive press campaign leads directly into a television campaign that will be screened to millions of viewers at peak times. This simple, yet telling, 45 second film is also available for use by approved Bulova stockists at their local cinemas. In addition to all this, all Bulova stockists will be supplied with quality display units and accessories to show off the new range at the point of sale. For full details of local cinema availability and display material—contact Rita Lewis or Judy Franks at Bulova, Lichfield (05432) 55211.

6

Faça o serviço militar em apenas 40 horas.

EMBRAER

7

8

INDUSTRIVÄGGEN SOM BLEV RUMSREN.

Electrolux Constructor

9

OLIVETTI LOGOS
REAL CALCULATORS
FOR REAL CALCULATORS

olivetti

Press advertisements
Annonces de presse
Zeitungs-Inserate

1a-c Brazil
AD Volkswagen do Brasil SA
AG Alcantara Machado, Periscinoto
Comunicaçoes Ltda
DIR (a-b) Buck Eugênio Curcio Filho,
(c) Joaquim Gonzalres de Oliveira
PHOTO (a) Andreas Heiniger,
(b) José Daloia Neto, (c) Meca
COPY (a-b) Adalberto d'Alambert
(c) Enio Basilio Rodrigues
Volkswagen Bug

2 Great Britain
AD Citroën Cars Ltd
AG Colman & Partners
DIR John Dodson
PHOTO Geoff Senior
COPY Peter Neeves
motor cars

3 Great Britain
AD Mercedes
AG Marsteller Ltd
DIR/DES Garry Denim
PHOTO Max Forsythe
COPY Mike Dennett
motor cars

4a-b United States
AD Yamaha Motors, US
AG Chiat/Day, Inc
DIR/DES Brenton Thomas
ILL Lamb & Hall
COPY Bernie Hafeli
Race Victory

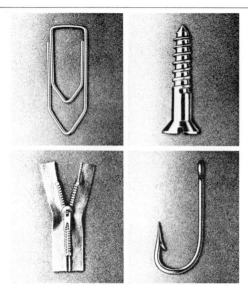

Quando uma idéia é boa, ela é definitiva.

Fusca. Bom hoje, bom amanhã, bom sempre.

1a

Fusca. Dinheiro aplicado, dinheiro recuperado.

Economia, investimento, garantia, até parecem palavras inventadas pelo Fusca. É que ele entende de poupança mais do que qualquer outro.

Veja só, você compra um Fusca hoje, pagando o menor preço inicial entre todos os carros nacionais.

E usa, usa, usa.

A mecânica Volkswagen refrigerada a ar é robusta e durável, com o menor consumo e o mais baixo custo de manutenção.

Amanhã você vai vender e o preço que você pagou volta direitinho às suas mãos. Quase sempre o dinheiro está até mais gordo.

Ponha tudo isso na coluna do lucro.

Mas não é só o dinheiro que conta. E a tranquilidade? Você sabe que o Fusca nunca está sozinho por esse

Brasil afora. E o prazer todinho que você teve?

Somando tudo, você verá por que as pessoas dizem que "quem sai de um Fusca sempre entra em outro". Entre no seu.

A marca que conhece o nosso chão.

1b

Depois da chave de casa, esta é a chave que os brasileiros mais carregam no bolso.

"Quantas vagas na garagem?"

Quando as pessoas se interessam por uma casa ou apartamento vão logo fazendo essa pergunta.

Eles estão reservando espaço para seus veículos Volkswagen. E fazem bem: desde que surgiu no Brasil, a Volkswagen produziu 4 milhões e quinhentos mil veículos.

Todos os meses, 40 mil pessoas em nosso país adquirem um veículo Volkswagen novinho. É um número maior do que a soma de todos os veículos de outras marcas.

Essa preferência é o resultado do profundo conhecimento que a Volkswagen tem das condições brasileiras. Nossos carros precisam ser resistentes, duráveis e

econômicos. A Volkswagen sempre foi fiel a esse princípio. É preciso fabricar veículos que satisfaçam a todos.

Para os que procuram racionalidade. E os que necessitam de espaço. Os que precisam de veículos duráveis para trabalhar. Os que gostam de esportividade. Os que optam pelo luxo. Aí estão o Fusca, Brasília, Variant II, Passat, Kombi.

A linha de veículos mais diversificada deste país. E que, certamente, em cada faixa de preço, oferece a opção mais gratificante pela compra.

Valorizados na hora de vender.

Gostar do Volkswagen brasileiro hoje é um hábito internacional. Nos últimos 5 anos a Volkswagen expor-

tou 250 mil veículos para mais de 50 países. E 300 mil motores para a Alemanha. Lá eles apreciam muito nossa marca.

Para oferecer tantas chaves, a Volkswagen assumiu grandes compromissos.

Aprimorando constantemente seus veículos. Desenvolvendo novos projetos. Concentrando a mais sofisticada linha de equipamentos de testes e pesquisas de toda a indústria automobilística.

Hoje, a responsabilidade de novos desenvolvimentos em motores refrigerados a ar, em todo o mundo, está nas mãos da Volkswagen do Brasil.

Tudo isso, para você ter um carro que é a extensão de sua própria casa.

E de manhã, atrasado para o trabalho, ao procurar a chave no bolso:

"Não está aqui! Devia estar! Onde você colocou as chaves do carro, mulher? Foram as crianças?"

Esse é o único problema.

A marca que conhece o nosso chão.

1c

3

4a

4b

1 Germany
AD Schröer KG
DIR Wolfgang Schulz, Hubert Maessen
DES Wolfgang Schulz
PHOTO Manufacturers
COPY Hubert Maessen
furniture, meubles,

2 India
AD Indian Tourist Board
AG Cherry Hedger Seymour
DIR Graham Cornthwaite
ILL John Claridge
COPY Geoff Seymour
tourism

3 United States
AD Axiom Designs
AG Gauger Sparks Silva
DIR/DES Walter Sparks
ILL Peter Olgivie
COPY John Stoddard
furnishings, meubles Möbel

4 Great Britain
AD Hornsea Pottery Co Ltd
AG Hornsea Pottery Design & Photographic
Studio
DES Francis Hart
ILL Trevor Richmond
tableware, poterie, porzellan

5 Great Britain
AD Rank Audio Visual—Pentax
AG Kirkwood Company
DIR Gregg Geist
COPY Peter Lorimer
cameras

6 Great Britain
AD Central Office of Information
AG Saatchi & Saatchi Garland-Compton
DIR James Woollett
Youth Opportunities Programme for
unemployed people, donner aux jeunes une
expérience du travail

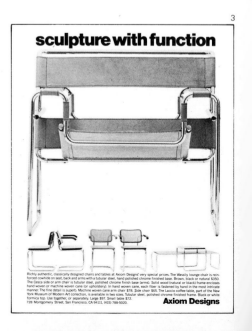

1

2

3

Live like a king: £750 a night.

india
ALLOW US TO SPOIL YOU

sculpture with function

Axiom Designs

7 Brazil
AD Rhodia SA
AG Alcantara Machado, Periscinoto
Communicaçoes Ltda
DIR Hans Haudenschild
PHOTO Miro
COPY E. loy Simões
Tergal sheets, draps de tergal

8 Denmark
AD Junckers Industrier A/S
AG Benton & Bowles
DIR/DES John Anderson
ILL Milling
COPY Elsebeth Høilund-Carlsen
new wooden floors, parquetage

CONCEPT
Oven to tableware, dishwasher and freezer safe.

HORNSEA

Hornsea Pottery Co Ltd, Hornsea, Yorkshire, England HU18 1UD *Telephone: 040 12 (Hornsea) 2161 Telex: 527279*

4

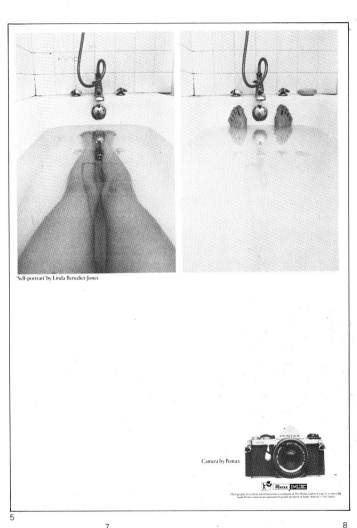

'Self-portrait' by Linda Benedict-Jones

Camera by Pentax

5

6

At 8, Joe was going to be an engine driver.

At 12, he was going to be a fireman.

At 14, he was going to be an electrician.

At 16, he's going nowhere. He's unemployed.

Phone (041) 331 2751. It's urgent. YOUTH OPPORTUNITIES PROGRAMME

7

Apresentamos os pilotos de prova dos lençóis Tergal.

Um bom lençol tem de estar preparado para tudo.
Para ser puxado, amassado, lavado e se manter sempre bonito. Sempre pronto pra ser usado. O lençol Tergal é assim. Resistente, dura uma eternidade. Apesar da brin-

cadeira exagerada da garotada. Macio, ele torna o sono ainda mais gostoso. Mais descansado. O lençol Tergal é fácil de lavar e não dá um pingo de trabalho para passar. O lençol Tergal é atual. Assim como você!

8

ET TRÆGULV HOLDER IKKE PÅ GAMMELT STØV.

Junckers trægulve. 100% ren natur.

1

2

3

4

5

7 Australia
AD E.R. Squibb & Sons
AG Flett Henderson & Arnold Graphic Design
DIR/DES Richard Henderson
pharmaceutical products

8 Great Britain
AD Pigments Division Ciba-Geigy (UK) Ltd
AG Ciba-Geigy Design Studio
DIR Brian Stones
DES/ILL Keith McMahon
COPY Janet Stewart
paint pigment for outdoor treatment, peinture
de couleurs pour traitement extérieur

9 Great Britain
AD White Satin Gin
AG Doyle, Dane, Bernbach Ltd
DIR/DES Michael Orr
PHOTO Phil Jude
COPY David Denton
gin

6

7

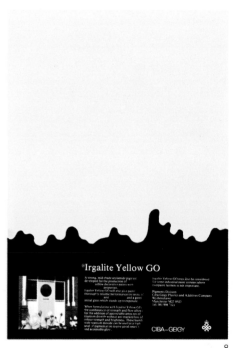

8

9

1

2

3

4

7 Great Britain
AD Rowntree Mackintosh
AG J. Walter Thompson
DIR/COPY Mike Trumble
ILL John Turner
peppermint chocolates, chocolate la la
menthe

kaasdroedel nr.1

Wat is dit?

Dit is een lekker stukje kaas. Er is zojuist een hapje uit
genomen door een jongetje dat onlangs z'n eerste
melktandje heeft verloren. Kaas is trouwens erg goed voor
kinder tanden. 't Is maar dat u het weet.

5a

kaasdroedel nr.7

Wat is dit?

Dit is een heel klein stukje, dat een heel lekker stukje
kaas van een heel hoge tafel pakt. Verstandig van dat jongetje,
want kaas is lekker en gezond. Wist u dat?

5b

kaasdroedel nr.3

Wat is dit?

Er is een lekker stukje kaas op de grond gevallen. U ziet hier hoe
een klein meisje zich bukt om het op te rapen. Kinderen
kunnen hun kaas brouwens maar beter nooit laten vallen, want
kaas is er om op te eten. Dat is goed voor ze. Goed om te weten...

5c

6a

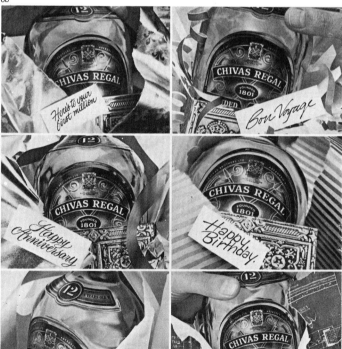

6b

Why wait for Christmas?

7

Mint, choc, mint, choc, mint,
choc, mint, choc, mint, choc, mint...

Press advertisements
Annonces de presse
Zeitungs-Inserate

1 Germany
AD Mustang Bekleidungswerke
AG Leonhardt & Kern
DIR Uli Weber
ILL Werner Bokelberg
COPY Brigitte Fussnegger
jeans

2 Israel
AD Rosi Shoes
AG Shem Design
shoes, chaussures

3 Italy
AD Florbath Profumi di Parma SpA
DIR Michele Gocche
DES Brozzi Giaeomo
ILL Zapelle
perfume

4 France
AD Parfums Yves Saint Laurent
AG MAFIA
DIR Philippe Sauter
ILL Sacha
COPY Philippe morand
bath salts, ligne pour le bain

6 France
AD Yves Saint Laurent Tricot
AG MAFIA
DIR Alexandre Wolkoff
ILL François Lamy
COPY Philippe Morand
Fashion, modes

5 United States
AD Jones New York
AG Murray H. Salit & Ass.
DIR Richard Gregory
DES Chuck Auerbach
PHOTO Bernard Vidal
fashions, modes

7 Great Britain
AD Creative Fragrances Ltd
AG Lovell & Rupert Curtis Ltd
DIR/DES Eric Dalton
PHOTO John Russell
COPY Mark Lovell
perfume

JONES NEW YORK

Fashion comes to life

Jones New York, 1411 Broadway, New York 10018

5

Yves Saint Laurent tricot. Comme un désir de renouveau.

YVES SAINT LAURENT
tricot

6

calandre

paco rabanne

7

**Hatschi
Gesundheit**

Bei Schnupfen hilft Rhinospray. Sprühen Sie es einfach in jedes Nasenloch: pffft pffft… Sofort wird Ihre Nase frei und der Kopf klar. Jetzt können Sie wieder richtig durchatmen. 7 bis 8 Stunden lang. Rhinospray ist zudem besonders mild und besonders gut verträglich. Nicht umsonst ist Rhinospray das am meisten verwendete Schnupfenspray. Sie bekommen es in Ihrer Apotheke.

Rhinospray zur Schleimhautabschwellung bei akutem und chronischem Schnupfen. Rhinospray ist für Erwachsene und Schulkinder bestimmt. Thomae Biberach/Riss

**Bei Schnupfen
RhinoSpray**

1

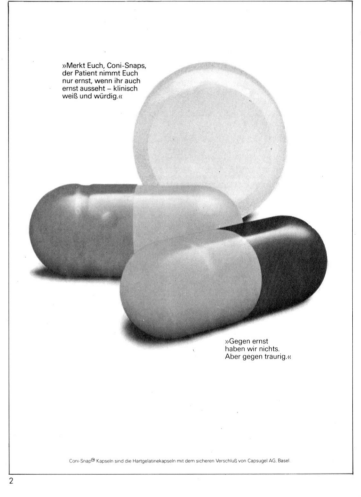

»Merkt Euch, Coni-Snaps, der Patient nimmt Euch nur ernst, wenn ihr auch ernst ausseht – klinisch weiß und würdig.«

»Gegen ernst haben wir nichts. Aber gegen traurig.«

Coni-Snap® Kapseln sind die Hartgelatinekapseln mit dem sicheren Verschluß von Capsugel AG. Basel.

2

3

For 25 years
'Thorazine' has helped to calm
chronic neurotic anxiety
and excessive agitation.*

A limited number of reproductions of this painting (8 1⁄2" x 11") suitable for framing are available by writing to Village Art Dept. E90, P.O. Box 7929, Philadelphia, Pa. 19101.

18 dosage forms and strengths · convenient, economical low dosage

Thorazine®
chlorpromazine
Tablets: 10, 25 or 50 mg. of the HCl

Smith Kline &French Laboratories
Division of SmithKline Corp · Philadelphia

SK&F

4

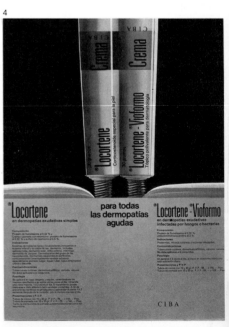

Locortene
en dermopatías exudativas simples

para todas
las dermopatías
agudas

Locortene -Vioformo
en dermopatías exudativas
infectadas por hongos o bacterias

7 Greece
AD Hellenika SA
AG K & K Univas Advertising Centre SARL
DIR/DES/ILL Agni Katzourakis
COPY Pelia Cambanellis
lipstick and nail varnish,

8 Denmark
AD General Foods
AG Young & Rubicam
DIR/DES Søren Parup
ILL Piotr
COPY Hans Djurhuus
coffee

Seven-Up Suikervrij spreekt een woord van dank.

Bas v.d. Kuit, fotograaf.
Je maakte echt schitterende foto's voor de campagne 1979 Seven-Up Suikervrij staat erop om van te watertanden!
Dat wordt weer imponerend reclame maken in de damesbladen. Full-colour nog wel! Bedankt, Bas!

J. Hemminga, winkelier.
U en uw collega's hebben het afgelopen jaar het beste beentje voorgezet bij het veroveren van de suikervrije markt!
U hebt op extra omzet gelet. Bedankt!
Zo blijft Seven-Up Suikervrij in de groei

Kees Leeuwenhart, assistent-bottelaar.
Helder begin van '79, Kees, Seven-Up Suikervrij groots samplen in de supermarkt. Zo tintelt Seven-Up Suikervrij zich wel een plaatsje naar de ijskast. Een sprankelend begin van het nieuwe jaar!

D. M. Vriezenveen, winkelier.
Samen met vele collega's gaf u Seven-Up Suikervrij en gewone Seven-Up consequent veel ruimte in het schap.
De ruimte die ze toekomt. En ook het rode display-materiaal wist u optimaal te gebruiken. Bedankt.
We hopen ook dit jaar weer op u te kunnen rekenen!

Monica de Waag, mannequin.
Dank je wel voor de gratis reclame die je maakte voor Seven-Up Suikervrij door er zo enthousiast over te vertellen aan iedereen die het maar horen wou.
Je denkt om je lijn en je blijft er lekker fris bij!

De dames Haagscheer, Knip, Vink en Schalie.
Nog steeds niet aan de suikervrije Seven-Up? Geeft niks, want dat betekent dat er voor Seven-Up met het rode etiket nog een enorme markt is weggegeven.
Een markt die in 1979 met kracht verder veroverd gaat worden!

Seven-Up Suikervrij. Met het rode etiket. Voor iedereen die op extra omzet let.

5

6

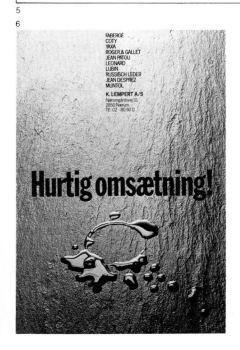

Hurtig omsætning!

FABERGÉ
COTY
YAXA
ROGER & GALLET
JEAN PATOU
LEONARD
LUBIN
RUSSISCH LEDER
JEAN DESPREZ
MUNTOL

K. LEMPERT A/S
Nærumgårdsvej 10,
2850 Nærum
Tlf.: 02 - 80 60 11

7

για το φθινόπωρο
απο τα χειλη ως τα νυχια seventeen

seventeen

8

1 Malet helt specielt.

Når man laver kaffe i kaffemaskine, drypper vandet langsommere ned over bønnerne end ved den traditionelle metode – den med kaffefilret og kedlen med kogende vand.
Derfor må en kaffe specielt til kaffemaskiner være anderledes end almindelig kaffe: Malet helt specielt, ristet lidt mørkere og blandet lidt anderledes.
Den grønne Gevalia er malet lidt grovere*).
Det bliver kaffen ikke mindre økonomisk af. Tværtimod. Det betyder, at vandet får den helt ideelle gennemløbstid, så kaffebønnerne kan udnyttes fuldt ud.
Så kommer hele den gode kaffesmag med ned i kaffekanden. Derfor får den nye, grønne Gevalia Deres kaffemaskine til at lave en endnu bedre kaffe.

*) Gevalia kaffe bliver hverken malet eller knust. Bønnerne skæres derimod i stykker af valser, som nøje kan justeres til den ønskede malingsgrad. På den måde sikres, at aromaen ikke går tabt i malingsprocessen.

GEVALIA
Den nye, grønne Gevalia får Deres kaffemaskine til at lave en endnu bedre kaffe.

1

"He wanted his belt back, so we made a deal."

"I think, somehow, I came out best."

The Jewellery Advisory Centre.
For gifts of gold visit any jeweller displaying this sign – your assurance of good jewellery and professional advice. The JAC, 44 Fleet Street, London E.C.4.

2

LOW TO MIDDLE TAR As defined by H.M. Government
H.M. Government Health Departments' WARNING:
CIGARETTES CAN SERIOUSLY DAMAGE YOUR HEALTH

3

Der Club ist der Club, der Groß und Klein auf charmante Art verführt: Hier zum Sichnäherkommen. Dort zum Alleinsein.

Und in paradiesischer Vielfalt locken reizvolle Versuchungen. Da gibt's Aktiv-Angebote für jede Kondition. Von Tennis bis Tauchen. Von Reiten bis Yoga. Hobby-Angebote verlocken zu kreativem Tun. Wie wär's zum Beispiel mal mit einem Töpferkursus? Und was unsere Köche täglich zaubern, ist die Verführung schlechthin. Aber, der Sport hält Sie ja bei Linie.

Alles im Club verführt dazu, mal so richtig auszuspannen und Mensch zu sein. Das reizt natürlich nicht Karl Jedermann. Weshalb Sie im Club auch nicht jedermann treffen. Sondern Menschen, die über Urlaub so denken wie Sie und wir. Was bekanntlich ungemein verbindet. Kommen Sie diesen Urlaub doch einfach mal mit. Ihr Reisebüro informiert Sie gern.

Club Méditerranée
Urlaub wie im Paradies – nur nicht so einsam.

Verführer-Club Méditerranée

4

Scottish Cashmere mit der einzigartigen Garantie: zu 100% in Schottland gesponnen und gestrickt.

Press advertisements
Annonces de presse
Zeitungs-Inserate

Mrs. Clark, of Buckinghamshire, spent 96 very happy hours knitting this sweater for you. 336 Sutter, San Francisco, (415) 986-4380.

Wilkes Bashford

1a

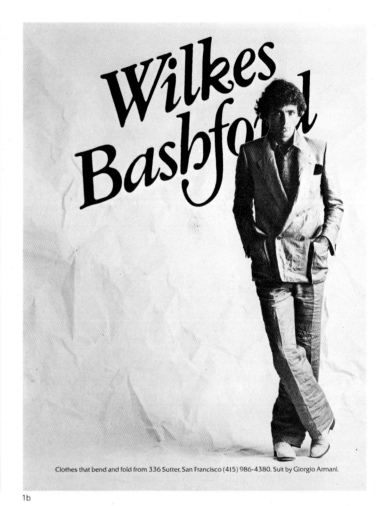

Clothes that bend and fold from 336 Sutter, San Francisco (415) 986-4380. Suit by Giorgio Armani.

1b

1c

Wilkes Bashford

The Prada Milano Collection. Luggage, handbags and small leather accessories to contain everything but your excitement, at 336 Sutter, San Francisco (415) 986-4380.

2

Die Pariserinnen sind vernarrt

BIJOUX
MURAT
Made in Paris

SCHMUCK IN WALZGOLD-DOUBLÉ, IN SILBER, IN GOLD 18 KARAT.
62, rue des Archives 75003 PARIS (France)

3

la informalidad de la elegancia
la palabra es **LEVI'S**

confeccionados con   INDIGO

7 Great Britain
AD Brook Advisory Centre
AG First City Advertising
DIR Peter Maisey
COPY Peter Maisey/Sue Hayman
birth control, contrôle de naissances,
Empfänisverhütung

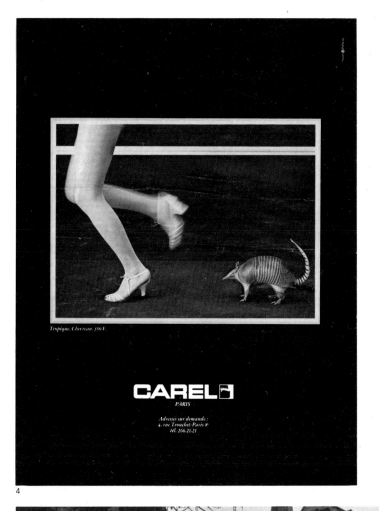

CAREL
PARIS

Tropique. Chevreau. 550 F.

Adresses sur demande :
4, rue Trouchet Paris 8ᵉ
tél. 266.21.21

4

‫.כלסאון" היא‬
‫נקודה על מפת היצרנים בעולם.‬
‫אך מבחינת זו מסומנים‬
‫52 נתיבי אספקה לכל רחבי-תבל.‬

‫52 מדינות‬
‫השוקת המשותפת‬
‫של פלסאון‬
‫מעגן/מיכאל‬

5

6

Paris, Rome or Somerset?

This is part of the new Piazza and Libra range of shoes from Clarks.
We think you'll agree they wouldn't look out of place in a

shop window on the Via Veneto or the Champs Elysees.
At least, not until you saw the price tag.
Not 60,000 lira, not 300 francs, but from £15·99. *Clarks*

7

'NO'

Like all methods of birth control
this only works if used every time.

Free birth control clinics for young people, all methods
of birth control, pregnancy testing and counselling.
Financed by the N.H.S. Five centres in London.

Brook
ADVISORY CENTRES
Ring 580 2991.

1a

Mary Quant introduces the Quarpet.

1b

1c

2

3

6 Germany
AD Bayerische Milchwirtschaft e.v.
AG Sainer Werbeagentur
DIR/DES Horst Fasel
PHOTO Urselmann
COPY Manfred Sainer
cream, crème, rahm

7 Germany
AD Ihring-Melchior Brauerei
AG SSM Werbeagentur/Studio Schlüter
DIR Harald Schlüter
ILL Harald Schlüter
COPY Jürgen Mehl
beer, biere

Ssh. Listen carefully. You can almost hear Toronto.

They say that when Toronto holds its festival of gourmet eating, drinking, dancing and music in June its the nearest thing to a ten-day European tour.

How come? Perhaps, in one way, its because Toronto isn't really a Canadian city at all. Its a city of the world. A place where people have come to settle from all the corners of the earth.

But in other ways, Toronto is very typical of a Canadian city.

Like Edmonton (where you can still pan for gold), like Vancouver (where you can get goose pimples swinging 230 feet over a canyon), like Montreal (where there are over 5,000 restaurants and where you can travel in a horse and carriage), Toronto is unique. And like most cities in Canada, the sort of scenery pictured above is on its doorstep.

This means you can have breakfast in your hotel in the city centre and be bobbing up and down on

a boat 176 feet below Niagara Falls by lunchtime. Spend the afternoon cutting a trail through country you thought you'd need an Indian scout to find. And be back in time for dinner and a show.

Once you've arrived in Canada its simple to do all the things you want to do. Whether that means hiring cars or canoes. Or staying in hotels or lakeside lodges.

Flights to Canada and hotel prices have never been better value. A double room in a comfortable motel

costing around £15 a night. And there are over 150 tours and package holidays available. A 6-day tour of Toronto, Montreal and Quebec costs about £110.

See your travel agent or write to Holidays in Canada, PO Box 9, London SW1Y 5DR for a free colour brochure and read about the land where the cry of the wild can still be heard over the hum of the cities.

Canada
Where nature had all its best ideas.

4

marantz.

5

6

7

Schlag rahm
die lecker-locker-leichte Krone!

Press advertisements
Annonces de presse
Zeitungs-Inserate

1 Brazil
AD R.J. Reynolds Tabacos do Brasil Ltda
AG Alcantara Machado
DIR Zbigniew Campioni
PHO Marcio Scavoni/Ernest Schauder
COP Claudio Correa
cigarettes

2 United States
AD Wisconsin Electric Power Company
AG Frankenberry Laughlin Bernstein &
Constable Inc
DIR/DES John Constable
ILL Bruce Bond
conservation, naturschutz

3 Sweden
AD IBM
AG Anderson & Lembke Vintergatan AB
DIR Frank Gabriele
DES Erik Grönlund
ILL Lasse Lie
COPY Bo Ahlberg
new office location, nouvel emplacement de
bureau, adressenänderung

4a-b United States
AD United Way
AG Cramer-Krasselt Co
DIR/DES John Constable, Cathy Sherwood
ILL Mike Jones
public service fund drive, parcours en aide
aux services publiques, wohlfahrts-sammlung

5 Great Britain
AD Morlands Coats
AG Cherry Hedger Seymour
DIR Graham Cornthwaite
PHOTO John Claridge
COPY Geoff Seymour
coats, manteaux, Mäntel

6 Holland
AD HAK
AG Intermarco-Farner B.V
DIR W. Schols
DES M. Bastin
ILL H.V.D. Heijden
COPY C. van Emdc Boas
conserves

1

2

3

4a

We're self centered.

Hard to believe?
Not really.
Each year the United Way helps improve the quality of life for hundreds of thousands of individuals throughout the Greater Milwaukee area.
And not just the handicapped, senile or poor.
In fact, most people who take advantage of United Way services are normal, healthy, hardworking folks. A lot like

your friends, neighbors and relatives. A lot like yourself.
Your United Way contribution supports programs like camping, scouting and neighborhood activities, homeowner's clinics and community planning . . . over 290 different programs and services in all.
So, this year, when you're asked to give, give for someone you know. Give for yourself.
Reach in. And reach out.
The United Way.

4b

Give at the office.
Like you said you did.

7 Great Britain
AD ICI Plastics
AG Stuart & Knight Ltd
DIR/DES Jo Czarnecki
ILL Jeremy Knight
Propafilm packaging film, film pour
l'emballage, plastikeinschrumpfung

8 India
AD Hindustan Organic Chemicals Ltd
AG Sista's Pvt Ltd
DIR/DES Niranjan Ghoshal
ILL Anand Mahajan
antipollution campaign, umweltschutz

when a luxury becomes a necessity

5

De natuur mag nog wel 'ns wisselvallig zijn. Hak niet. Hak wenst alleen het beste van het goede in z'n potten.

Heel kritisch kiest Hak de eerste keuze uit al die groenten, al dat fruit. De rest verdient de naam Hak niet.

U verwacht topkwaliteit van Hak. Die krijgt u. Altijd. Het hele jaar door. Daar kunt u van op aan.

Zelfs van een goede bonenoogst komt alleen eerste kwaliteit in een pot van Hak.

Hak... je weet wat je koopt.

6

PROPAFILM

GREAT COVER UP STORY!

Fresh tasting products
'Propafilm', with its excellent moisture barrier properties and strong, easily made heat seals, ensures the maintenance of quality for long periods.

Durable packs
Damage from sharp edged products is minimised by toughness and high puncture resistance. The protection of 'Propafilm' can be relied upon even at sub-zero temperatures.

Attractive packs
'Propafilm' can be printed at high speeds and the excellent surface qualities of the film ensure high gloss, clarity, sparkle and good handling.

Good packaging performance
The good slip and anti-static properties of 'Propafilm' provide easy and efficient packaging for an extensive range of products on a wide variety of automatic wrapping machines.

Uncreased packs
Due to its high dimensional stability, 'Propafilm' is not affected by humidity

and temperature variations, giving wrinkle and shrink-proof packs.

Reduced packaging costs
The low density (high yield) of 'Propafilm' provides economical advantages and, due to its excellent barrier properties, it can often be employed in thicknesses lower than those of other films.

ICI is Europe's largest producer of oriented polypropylene films with grades to meet a wide range of packaging requirements.

'Propafilm' C – a two-sided PVdC coated, heat-sealable film.
'Propafilm' M – a co-extruded, all-polyolefine, heat-sealable film.
'Propafilm' O – an uncoated film.

For further information on 'Propafilm' please contact:
Packaging Films Sales Dept.,
ICI Plastics Division
PO Box 6, Welwyn Garden City,
Herts. AL7 1HD
Tel: Welwyn Garden 23400
Telex: 264251

ICI–a world leader in packaging films

PPF31

7

POLLUTION. It's not a problem we can live with. Not for long.

So much has been said about pollution in the past few years that a lot of people have started accepting it as a fact of life.
In fact, it's quite the opposite. And unless we do something about it, now, the consequences will be grave.
In India, it has not reached the same devastating proportions as elsewhere around the world. We've got to fight it, while we've still got the time.
At Hindustan Organic Chemicals, we're very concerned about the problem. And constantly working on it, coming out with practical solutions.
Our Pollution Control Programme will cost us about Rs. 200 lakhs by the time it's through. So far, we've already invested Rs. 98 lakhs towards projects of immediate urgency. For instance, we've laid down a 9-km long pipeline to carry away effluents to a faraway creek.
We've erected a 55-metre high stack gas chimney with a Brink Mist Eliminator to drastically reduce acid mist emission into the atmosphere.
A specially designed Flaking Unit in our Benzene Hexachloride Plant, now under commissioning trials, will make the effluent discharge clean and safe.
We are planning to instal a Double Conversion Double Absorption (DCDA) System to reach close to zero emission.
What's more, we're soon setting up a very efficient Detoxification System that will greatly help us fight pollution. We've also set up a Recovery Plant which takes in the effluents and from them extracts a toxic ingredient—a chemical that is also a much needed, commercially important product—Resorcinol.
Actually, this has even earned us the All India Manufacturers Organisation Award for the best performance in the recovery and recycling of pollutants from effluents.
The fact remains that what we're really concerned about is not winning awards for fighting pollution. But fighting pollution and winning. And we're fighting it as if our lives are at stake. Because they are. All our lives.

HINDUSTAN ORGANIC CHEMICALS LIMITED
(A Government of India Enterprise) Regd. Office: P.O. Rasayani 410 207, Dist. Kulaba, Maharashtra. Tel: 21—26, 57—60. Telegram: 'HINORCH' RASAYANI.

8

Bookjackets
Chemises de Livres
Buchumschläge

1 Germany
AD Wolfgang Hölker Verlag
DES Wolfgang Hölker
ILL Antje Vogel

2 Germany
AD Letraset Deutschland
AG Christof Gassner
DES Christof Gassner
Catalogue for Typography Exhibition

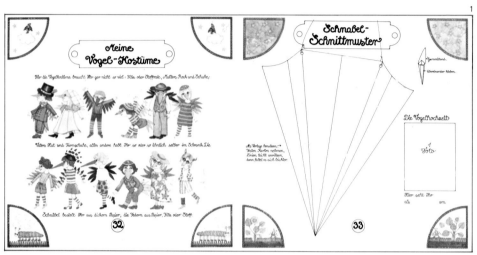

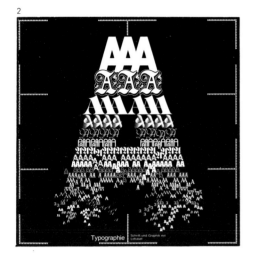

Typefaces
Caractères
Schrifttypen

1a-c Great Britain
AD Face Type Ltd
DIR (a) Pat Hickson (b, c) J.M. Charve
DES Pat Hickson
(a) 'Kitterland', (b) 'Appleyard' (c) Appleyard
Extra Bold'

2 Holland
AD Eduard Mlinar
DIR/DES Eduard Mlinar
'Nailer'

3 Great Britain
AD Alphabet Photosetting
DIR Dave Farey
DES Bernard Allum

4a-c Great Britain
AD Film Composition
AG Film Composition
DIR Ed Cleary
COP Ed Cleary
advertises film setting services

4d, e United States
AD International Typeface Corporation
AG Film Composition
DES Colin Brignall
typeface, Italia medium and Italia bold

4f-4h United States
AD International Typeface Corporation
AG Film Composition
DES Herman Zapf
Zapf International series light, medium, demi

4i-l United States
AD International Typeface Corporation
AG Film Composition
DES Tony Staus
ITC Garamond series, Garamond light, light
condensed, Book condensed, Bold
condensed

Kitterland

ABCDEFGHIJKLMNOPQRSTUVWXYZ
aabcdeffghijklmnopqrstuvwxyz
ß£1234567890&?!.,:;‘’()
ÆŒØæœøffffflfrftfuffifflffr

1a

Appleyard

ABCDEFGHIJKLMNOPQRSTUVWXXYZ
abcdefghijklmnopqrstuuvwxxyz
£1234567890ß&.,:;‘’!?()[]

1b

Appleyard Extra Bold

ABCDEFGHIJKLMNOPQRSTUVWXXYZ
abcdefghijklmnopqrstuuvwxxyz
£1234567890&.,:;‘’!?()[]

1c

AABCDEFGHIJKLM
NOOPQQRSSTUVWUXXYYZ
£1234567890
&(.,!?)

2 | 3

abcdefghijklmnopqrstuvwxyz
ABCDEFGHIJKLMNOPQRSTUVWXYZ
1234567890

4d

abcdefghijklmnopqrstuvwxyz
ABCDEFGHIJKLMNOPQRSTUVWXYZ
1234567890

4e

Garamond Condensed

Filmcomposition.

4a

ITC Garamond Book Condensed

Designed by Tony Stan
between 1975 and 1977 for ITC, New York.
Now available for diatronic filmsetting from
Filmcomposition.

Specimen setting Garamond Book Condensed 11 key, on 11 feed W. spacing
Excellence in typography is the result of nothing more tha
n an attitude. Its appeal comes from the understanding use
d in its planning; the designer must care. In contemporary
advertising the perfect integration of design elements ofte
n demands unorthodox typography. It may mean the use o
f compact spacing, minus leading, unusual sizes and weight
s; whatever is necessary to improve appearance and impac
t. Stating specific principles or guides on the subject of typo
graphy is difficult. No rule is useful if it inhibits or restricts t
he ultimate purpose of the design. Fine typography is the r

Specimen setting Garamond Book Condensed 11 key, on 11 feed W. plus spacing
Excellence in typography is the result of nothing more
than an attitude. Its appeal comes from the understandi
ng used in its planning; the designer must care. In cont
emporary advertising the perfect integration of design
elements often demands unorthodox typography. It ma
y mean the use of compact spacing, minus leading, unu
sual sizes and weights; whatever is necessary to impro
ve appearance and impact. Stating specific principles or
guides on the subject of typography is difficult. No rule
is useful if it inhibits or restricts the ultimate purpose of

We're
Filmcomposition.
It must
look good.
Filmcomposition.

4b

abcdefghijklmnopqrstuvwxyz
ABCDEFGHIJKLMNOPQRSTUVWXYZ
1234567890

4f

abcdefghijklmnopqrstuvwxyz
ABCDEFGHIJKLMNOPQRSTUVWXYZ
1234567890

4g

abcdefghijklmnopqrstuvwxyz
ABCDEFGHIJKLMNOPQRSTUVWXYZ
1234567890

4h

4c

abcdefghijklmnopqrstuvwxyz
ABCDEFGHIJKLMNOPQRSTUVWXYZ
1234567890

4i

abcdefghijklmnopqrstuvwxyz
ABCDEFGHIJKLMNOPQRSTUVWXYZ
1234567890

4j

abcdefghijklmnopqrstuvwxyz
ABCDEFGHIJKLMNOPQRSTUVWXYZ
1234567890

4k

abcdefghijklmnopqrstuvwxyz
ABCDEFGHIJKLMNOPQRSTUVWXYZ
1234567890

4l

Typefaces
Caractères
Schrifttypen

1 Great Britain
AD Filmcomposition
DIR Colin Craig
DES Ed Cleary
photosetting services

2 Germany
AG Christof Gassner Grafik-Design
DES Christof Gassner

3 Great Britain
AD Letraset International Ltd
AG Letraset Studios
DIR Tony Bowler
DES David Prout/Terry Russell
new 'Letragrafika' instant lettering

4 Great Britain
AD Letterbox Ltd
DIR/DES Bob Owen
photosetting catalogue

5 United States
AD International Typeface Corp.
AG U & lc International
DIR/DES Herb Lubalin
cover for typographical magazine

6a, b Canada
AD Hunter Brown Ltd
AG Burns, Cooper, Hynes Ltd
DIR Robert Burns
DES Ann Ames
ILL Heather Cooper
promotional postcards for filmsetting
company

Graphic services portfolio

Letterbox Ltd., 1 Basire Street, Islington N1 8PN

4a

Century Schoolbook Bold (CS 65)

Letterbox

4b

5

A Letter from Hunter Brown

24 Ryerson Avenue
Toronto, Ontario
M5T 2P3

PAR AVION   AIR MAIL   VIA AEREA

Hand Lettering from Hunter Brown

6

7

Compugraphic hat ITC Benguiat Condensed

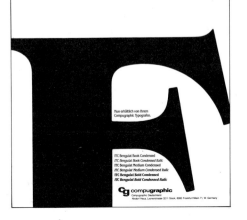

Nun erhältlich von Ihrem
Compugraphic Typografen.

ITC Benguiat Book Condensed
ITC Benguiat Book Condensed Italic
ITC Benguiat Medium Condensed
ITC Benguiat Medium Condensed Italic
ITC Benguiat Bold Condensed
ITC Benguiat Bold Condensed Italic

cg compugraphic
Compugraphic Deutschland
Niedorf Haus, Lorenzstrasse 32 H. Stadt, 6000 Frankfurt/Main 71, W. Germany

Bookjackets
Chemises de Livres
Buchumschläge

1a-c Great Britain
AD Routledge & Kegan Paul Ltd
DIR/DES/ILL John Gibbs

2 Great Britain
AD Associated Book Publishers
DIR/DES/ILL Adam Yeldham

3 France
AD Editions Fleurus
DIR Yves Setton
DES Jean-Claude Denis

4 France
AD François Maspero
AG Roman Cieslewicz
DIR/DES/ILL Roman Cieslewicz

5 Spain
AD Euros Editorial
AG C. Rolando Asociados
DIR Roberto Dosil, Carlos Rolando
DES Roberto Dosil
PHOTO Sergio Hernandes

6 Brazil
AD Livraria Cultura Editora
AG Schwab & Noro
DIR Alfredo Aquino
DES/ILL Alfredo Aquino
COPY Livaria Cultura Editora

7 Canada
AD Tundra Books
AG Rolf Harder & Associates
DIR/DES Rolf Harder
ILL William Kureler
COPY Ivan Franks

1a

1b

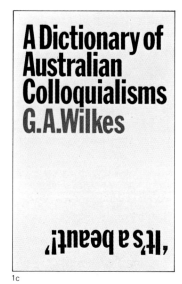

1c

2

3

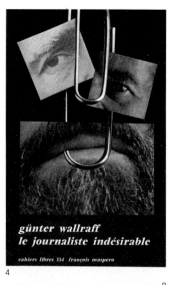

4

5

9

6

10

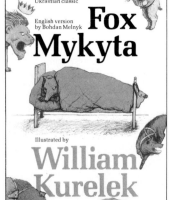

7

8

9

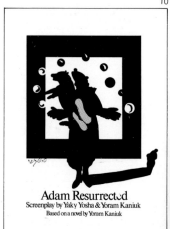

11a

11b

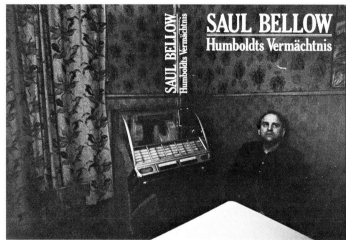

11c

11d

12a

12b

13

14

15a

15b

Bookjackets
Chemises de Livres
Buchumschläge

1a-b Great Britain
AD Penguin Books
DIR (a) David Pelham, John Carrod
    (b) David Pelham
DES (a) John Carrod (b) John Carrod
PHOTO Trefor Ball (b) John Carrod

2 Great Britain
AD Futura Books
AG Roman and Moira Buj
DIR Patrick Mortemore
DES/ILL Roman Buj

3a-b Great Britain
AD Transworld Publishers Ltd (Corgi Books)
DIR John Munday
DES Sushma Baqaya
ILL (a) Paul Sample (b) Ken Laidlaw

4 United States
AD Harcourt, Brace, Jovanvich
AG Wendell Minor Design
DIR Harris Lewine
ILL/DES Wendell Minor

5 Spain
AD Circulo de Lectores s.a.
AG/DES Jabier Noguera

6a-c Italy
AD Mondadori Editore
AG Servizio Grafico Editoriale
DIR Bruno Binosi
DES (a) Ferenc Pinter
    (b, c) Ferrucio Bocca

1a

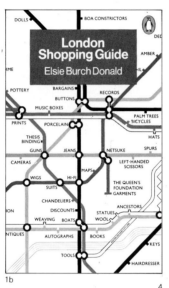

1b

2

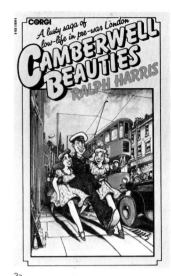

3a

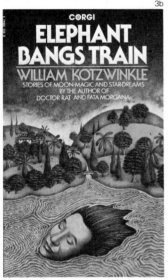

3b

4

5

6a

6b

6c

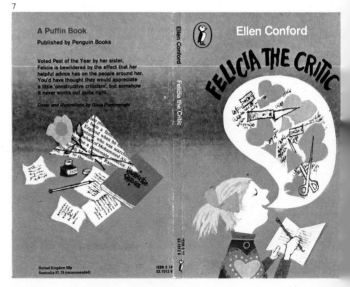

7

7 Great Britain
AD Puffin Books
DIR Doreen Scott
DES Gioia Fiammenghi
book jacket

8 Netherlands
AD Peter Loeb
DES Ian Cremer

9 Germany
AD Büchergilde Gutenberg
DES/ILL Hennes Maier

10a-c Great Britain
AD Transworld Publishers Ltd (Corgi Books)
DIR John Munday
DES Bipin Patel
ILL James Jackson
MODEL BY Ken Gillham
book jackets

11a-b Italy
AD Mondadori Editore
AG Servizio Grafico Editoriale
DIR Bruno Binosi
DES Ferenc Pinter

12a-c United States
AD (a-b) Dodd, Mead & Co,
   (b-c) Houghton Mifflin Co
AG Wendell Minor Design
DIR (a) Peter Weed, (b-c) Louise Noble
DES/Ill Wendell Minor

8

9

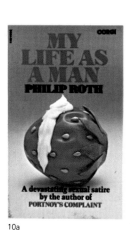

10a

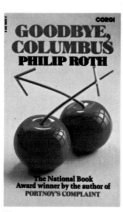

10b

10c

11a

11b

12a

12b

12c

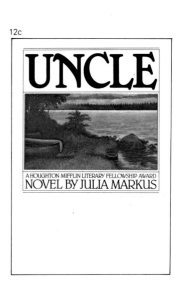

Bookjackets
Chemises de Livres
Buchumschläge

1a-b United States
AD (a) Teachers College Press,
(b) Family Services Ass.
AG Ner Beck Design
DIR (a) Mel Berk, Mary Allison
(b) Jackie Atkins
DES/ILL Ner Beck

2 Great Britain
AD Collins Publishers
DES Nick Bantock

3 United States
AD Franklin Watts
DIR Judie Mills
DES Frances Jetter

4 United States
AD Harcourt, Brace,
DIR Harris Lewine
ILL Carl Fischer

5a Great Britain
AD Routledge & Kegan Paul Ltd
DIR/DES/ILL John Gibbs

5b Great Britain
AD Routledge & Kegan Paul Ltd
DIR John Gibbs
DES John Gibbs and Vivien Kersey

1a

1b

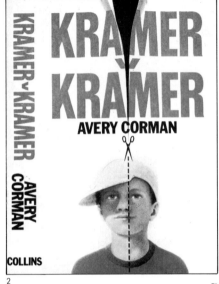

2

5b

3

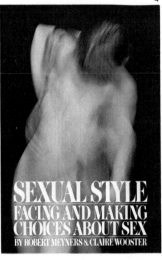

4

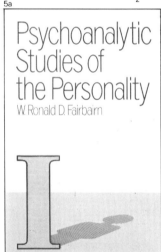

5a

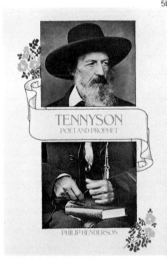

6

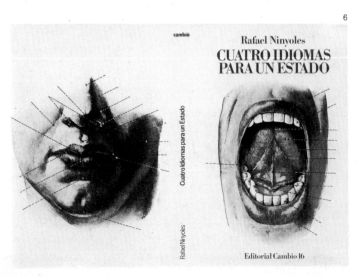

7

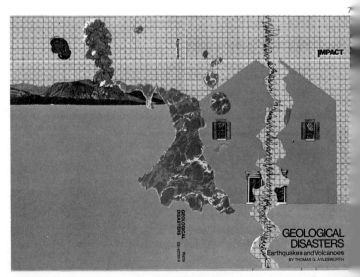

5 Spain
AD Editorial Cambio 16
AG C. Rolando Asociados
DIR/DES R. Dosu, C. Rolando

7 United States
AD Franklin Watts
DIR Judie Mills
DES Frances Jetter

8 Great Britain
AD Barrie & Jenkins
AG Roman and Moira Buj
DIR Brian Nichols
DES Roman Buj

9a-b Great Britain
AD Associated Book Publishers
DIR/DES Adam Yeldham
ILL (a) Chris Morre, (b) Barbara Kay

10a-b United States
AD University of Chicago Press
DIR (a) Patricia Burdett (b) Richard Pace
DES (a) Ted Lacey (b) Richard Pace

9a

9b

10a

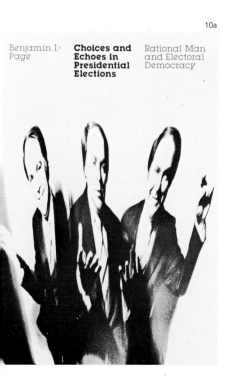

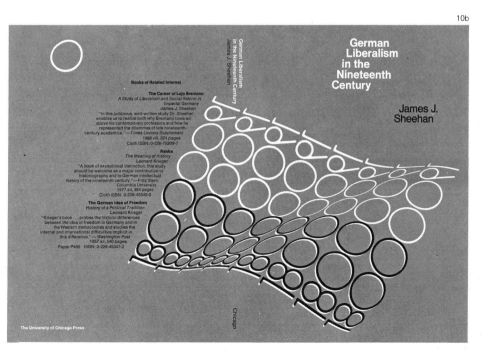

10b

Bookjackets
Chemises de Livres
Buchumschläge

1a-b France
AG Gallimard
DIR Pierre Marchand
ILL Jean Claverie
children's book, livre d'enfants

2a-c Great Britain
AD Eel Pie Publishing
AG Insel Verlag
DES/ILL Monika Beisner
address book for children, carnet d'addresses
pour les enfants, Addressenbuch für Kinder

3 Great Britain
AD The MacMillan Company
DES Ron and Atie Van der Meer

4 Great Britain
AD Writers & Readers Co-op Publishing
DIR/DES/ILL Oscar Zarate
COPY Arnold Wesker

5a-b Great Britain
AD Hamish Hamilton Ltd
DES/ILL Raymond Briggs

6a-b Great Britain
AD Kestrel Books
DES John Astrop
book of boardgames

1a

1b

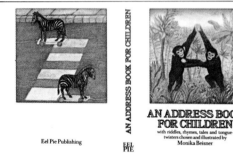

2a

2b

2c

3

4

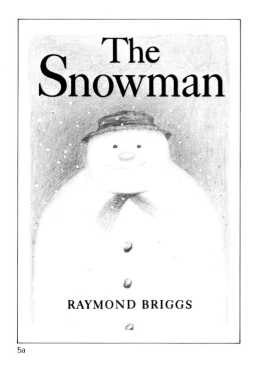

5a

5b

6a

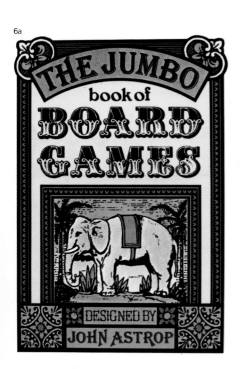

6b

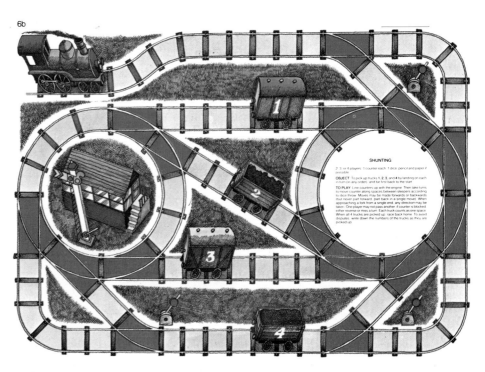

Bookjackets
Chemises de Livres
Buchumschläge

1a-d United States
AD American Book Company
AG Steve Bernstein Design
DIR Bill Dippel
DES Steve Bernstein
elementary education reading textbooks,
livres de lecture pour education élémentaire,
Lesebücher

2a-c Great Britain
AD W.H. Smith & Son
AG Guyatt/Jenkins Ltd
DIR/DES/ILL Ian Wright
COPY Ian Wright
staff training manual, manuel pour
l'instruction du personnel

3a-b Australia
AD Australian National University Press
AG ANV Graphic Design
DIR/DES/ILL (a) Adrian Young
             (b) Stephen Cole, Adrian
                 Young
ILL (b) Kirsty Morrison

4 United States
AD Doubleday & Company
AG Goslin/Barnett Inc
DIR Rallou Hamshaw
DES David Barnett

5a-c Japan
AD Yugakusha Publications, Inc
AG AN Creative Co Ltd
DIR Tatsundo Hayashi
DES/ILL (a) Yukio Akiyama
        (b, c) Tatsundo Hayashi

6a-b Great Britain
AD Wm. Collins Sons & Co
DIR/DES Ian McIlroy
PHOTO Gus Wylie
COPY The Hebrides

1a

1b

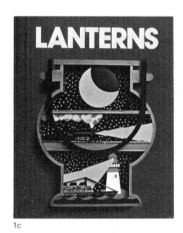

1c

1d

2a

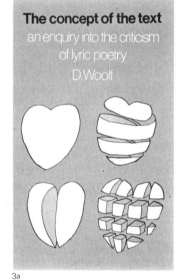

3a

3b

4

2b

2c

5a

5b

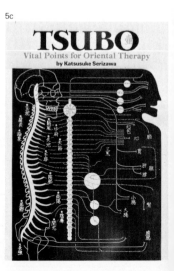

5c

7 Great Britain
AD The British Phonographic Industry Ltd
AG Brooks Design Partnership
DIR/DES Barry Brooks
ILL Brian Robbins
annual review of British record industry,
revue annuelle de l'industrie du disque de
Grande Bretagne, jahresbericht für
Grammophonindustrie

8 Germany
AD Büchergilde Gütenberg
DIR/DES Hennes Maier

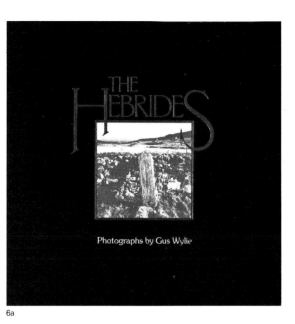

6a

Daytrippers, Rhum

6b

7

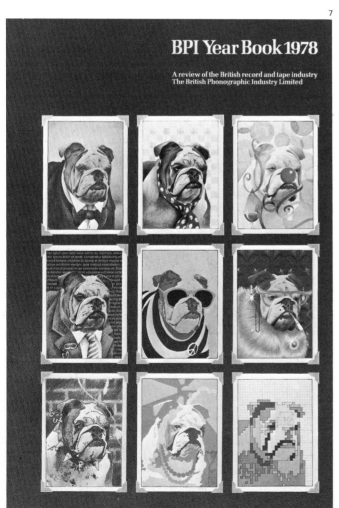

8

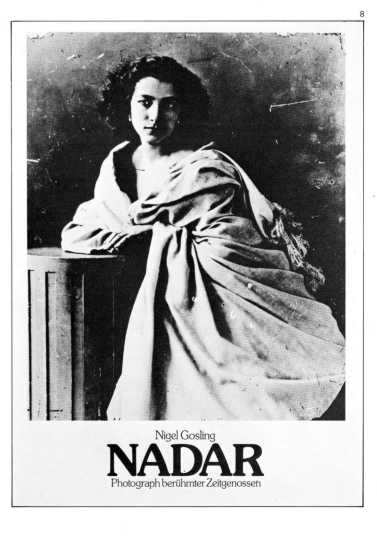

Postage-stamp designs
Dessins de Timbres-poste
Briefmarken Entwürfe

1 Switzerland
DES Celestino Piatti

2a-b Canada
DES Reinhard Derreth

3a-b Netherlands
DES Babs van Bely

4 United Nations
DES A. Glaser

5 United States
DES Paul Calle

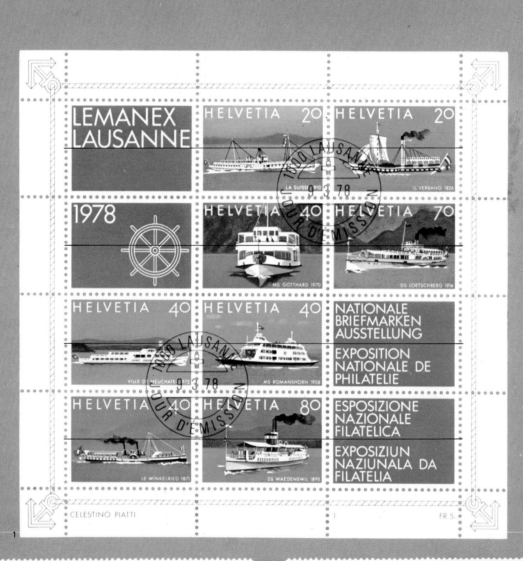

2a

2b

6 Monaco
DES Mlle Martin
Engraver: Larriviere

7a-b Hungary
DES János Kass

8 Poland
Children's Drawings

9 Great Britain
DES Edward Hughes

10a-b Antigua
AG Intergovernmental Philatelic Corporation
DES Mark Rubin

11a-b Liechtenstein
DES Roberto Altmann

12 Sweden
DES Petter Petterson

13 Portugal
DES Jose Luis Tinoco

14 India
DES Government Studies

15 German Federal Republic
DES Karl-Oskar Blase

3a

3b

4

5

6

7a

7b

8

9

10a

10b

11a

11b

12

13

14

15

Postage-stamp designs
Dessins de Timbres-poste
Briefmarken Entwürfe

1a

2a

2b

3

4

5a

6

7

8

9a

10a

11a

11b

11c

12

10b

13

5b

14

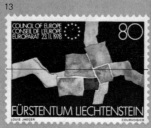

15 Sweden
DES Tom Hultgren

16a-b Jersey
DES Jennifer Toombs

17a-b Venezuela
DES (a) M.F. Nedo
　　(b) Gerd Leufert

18 Belgium
DES J. Malvaux/Dechy

19 Canada
DES Don Haws

20a-b Bulgaria
DES Stephan Kantscheff

21 St Helena
AG/DES Crown Agents
DES Clive Abbott

22 Republic of South Africa
DES H. Botha

23 Botswana
AG Crown Agents
DES M.F. Bryan

15

16a-b

5c

1b

10c

17 a

18

9b

19

11d

11e

20a

20b

17b

21

22

23

Postage-stamp designs
Dessins de Timbres-poste
Briefmarken Entwürfe

1a-b Italy
DES (a) Francesco Tulli
      (b) G. Pirotta

2 United States
DES Bradbury Thompson

3 India
AG/DES Indian Government Studios

4 San Marino
AG/DES Courvoisier

5 Mexico
DES Gad Almaliah

6a-b Switzerland
DES (a) Hans Erni
      (b) Klaus Öberli

7 Finland
DES Paavo Huovinen

8 Liechtenstein
DES Joseph Schädler

9 Venezuela
DES Gerd Leufert

10 Trinidad and Tobago
AG Crown Agents
DES Leslie Curtis
ILL Ruben Chong/Dunston Williams

11 Hong Kong
AG Crown Agents
DES Post Office Studios

12 German Federal Republic
DES Bruno K. Wiese

13a-e Israel
DES (a-c) A. Hecht
      (d) A. Hecht
      (e) D. Pessah/S. Ketter

14 Brazil
DES Ary Fagundes

15 Netherlands
DES Hans Kruit

1a

2

3

4

5

6a

7

8

9

10

6b

11

12

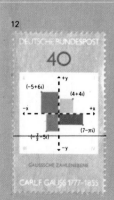

13a

13b

13c

14

16 Malta
AG Malta Post Office
DES Tazza Tadonja

17a-d Mexico
DES (a) Jorge Canales
     (b) Gad Almaliah
     (c) R. Davidson
     (d) Lala Silva

18a-b Canada
DES Stuart Ash

19 Japan
DES Niko Tsukada/Yoshiaka Kirkuchi

20a-b Austria
DES Otto Stefferl

21 United Nations
DES Cafiero Tomei

22 Tanzania
AG Crown Agents

13d

1b

15

16

17a

18a

18b

19

17b

17c

17d

20 a

20b

21

13c

22

Postage-stamp designs
Dessins de Timbres-poste
Briefmarken Entwürfe

1 Bulgaria
DES Weni Kantardjewa

2a-d Venezuela
DES (a) Government Studio
     (b, d) Gerd Leufert
     (c) M.F. Nedo

3a-g German Federal Republic
DES (a) Elisabeth von Janota Bzowski
     (b) Prof. Gunter H. Magnus
     (c) Dieter Urban
     (d) Prof. Herbert Stelzer
     (e) Fritz Hasse
     (f, g) Hella & Heinz Schillinger

4 Ireland
DES/ILL Louis Le Brocquy

5 India
DES Government Studios

6 Switzerland
DES Walter Haettenschweiler

7a-c Netherlands
DES (a) Ab Gratama/Sjoerd de Vries
     (b) Bart de Groot
     (c) Wim Crouwel

8a-b United States
DES (a) Dolly Tingel
     (b) Ben Somoroff

9 Colombia
AG/DES De la Rue Studios

10 Indonesia
DES R. Soetedjo

11a-b Czechoslovakia
DES (a) Anna Podzemna
     (b) Joseph Liesler

12a-b Samoa i Sisifo
AG Crown Agents
DES John Waddington Studios

13 Australian Antarctic Territories
AG Australian Stamp Bureau
DES Ray Honisett

1

2a

2b

3a

3b

2c

4

5

3c

6

7a

7b

7c

8a

3d

8b

2d

8c

9

10

14 Falkland Islands
AG Crown Agents
DES Glyn Hutchins

15 Canada
DES Tom Bjarnason

16 Mexico
DES J. Canales

17 Brazil
DES Lucia T.V. Ramos

18 Jersey
AG Crown Agents
DES A. Theobald

19 Jamaica
AG Crown Agents
DES David Bowen

20 Sweden
DES Sture Karlsson

21 New Zealand
DES R.M. Conly

22 Great Britain
DES Peter Newcombe

11a

11b

3e

12a

12b

13

14

15

16

17

18

3f

19

3g

20

21

22

Trademarks
Marques
Schutzmarken
Letterheads
en têtes
Briefköpfe

1a-c Great Britain
AD Pinewood Film Studios
AG Peter Proto Associates
DIR Peter Proto
DES Peter Proto and Jon Bodsworth
stationery and Christmas card for 'Superman'
film, carte de Noël pour le film 'Superman',
Briefpapier für 'Superman' Filmgesellschaft

2 France
AG Hand-lettering Studio
AG Claude Mediavilla
DES Claude Mediavilla
various logos and trademarks, marquees
variés, verschiedenc Wahrenzeichen

Alexander Salkind

Pierre Spengler

Ilya Salkind

1a

1b

1c

Trademarks
Marques
Schutzmarken

1 Spain
AD OIGA! (Studio)
AG OIGA!
DIR/DES Juan Torregaray
COPY Iñigo Baragaña
advertising studio, studio de publicité,
Reklamebüro

2 Israel
AD American Israel Bank
AG Ounat/Karmon/Shifrin/Na'aman
DIR/DES Yak Molho
symbol for 15th anniversary of the bank,
15ème anniversaire de la banque, 15.
jubilänm einer Bank

6 Great Britain
AD Race Furniture Ltd
AG Unit Five Design Ltd
DIR/DES Gus Hunnybun
modular furniture, meubles modulaires,
modulär-möbel

7 United States
AD Desire Custom Jewelry Design
AG Nicholas Sinadinos Design
DIR/DES Nicholas Sinadinos
custom jewelry design firm,
bijouterie sur commande,

3 Italy
AD Galvani ceramiche
AG Studio de Santis
DIR/DES Alfredo de Santis
ceramic factory

8 United States
AD Al Marc Koch
AG Alan Wood Graphic Design
DIR/DES Alan Wood
unisex haircutter, salon de coiffure homme et
femme, Unisex Friseur

4 Spain
AD Fernando Medina
DIR/DES Fernando Medina
promotional brochure, brochure de promotion

5 South Africa
AD Afship
AG Adam (Pty.) Ltd
DIR/DES Clive Gay
transport company

9, 10 France
AD Fock en Stock Magazine
AG Jean Larcher
DIR Laurent Buvry/Paul Putti
DES Jean Larcher
magazine titles

11 Great Britain
AD BBC TV
DES Tim Harvey
T-shirt motif advertising TV musical

12 Mexico
AD Recon S.A. de S.V.
AG Rion & Ezquerro Assoc.
DIR Fernando Rion
DES Rion & Esquerro
engine reconstruction, reconstruction des
moteurs, Motorenreparatur

13 Great Britain
AD East Anglian Soft Toys
AG Bloy Eldridge
DES Robert Custance
soft toy manufacturers, fabricant de jouets en
peluche, Puppenfabrik

14 Canada
AD Hunter Brown Ltd
AG Burns, Cooper, Hynes Ltd
DIR Robert Burns
DES Robert Burns, Ann Ames
typesetters

15 Great Britain
AD Gorilla Grip Ltd
AG Unit Five Design Ltd
DIR Gus Hunnybun
DES Keith Pickton
automative products company

16 Hong Kong
AD Edmund Metal Works Ltd
AG The Group Advertising Ltd
DIR/DES Kan Tai-keung
metal furniture

17 United States
AD Wisconsin
AG Hayward Blake & Company
DIR Hayward Blake
DES Gail Aalund

18 Spain
AD Dispotex, SA
AG José Ros González
DIR José Ros González
surgical material, matériel chirurgique,
verbandsstoffe

19 United States
AD Milwaukee Art Center
AG Frankenberry Laughlin Bernstein &
Constable Inc
DIR/DES John Constable
fund drive, parcours pour aide de fonds,
Geldsammlunig für Kunstzeutrum

20 Japan
AD Japan Ad-Art Inc
AG Japan Ad-Art Inc
DIR/DES/ILL Masahiro Oishi
package design studio, studio de dessins
d'emballage, Verpackungsentwurf

Trademarks
Marques
Schutzmarken

1 Canada
AD Grand Prix du Canada
AG Rolf Harder & Associates
DIR/DES Rolf Harder
Formula 1 Grand Prix race, grand Prix

6 United States
AD Senior Jesuits Program
AG Edward Hughes Design
DIR/DES Edward Hughes

2 Japan
AD Isetan Department Store
AG Nippon Design Center
DIR Kenzo Nakagawa
DES Kenzo Nakagawa/Hiro Nobuyama
department store, magasin, Warenhaus

7 United States
AD Archdiocesan Councils
AG Gerry Kano Design
DIR/DES Gerry Kano
ILL Tina Tomiyama
promoting understanding within the
community, pour l'entente dans la
communauté, Harmonie zwischen
Religionsgemeinschaften

3 Denmark
AD Bruun & Sørensen Engineering Company
AG Niels Hartmann
DES Niels Hartmann
engineering company, Ingenieur

8 Austria
AD Chemometall
AG Badian & Weinblatt
DIR/DES Joey Badian
recycling firm, usine de reciclage,
Wiederverwendung

4 United States
AD Council of Services for Families and
Children
AG Ner Beck Design
DIR Jeff Hantover
DES Ner Beck

9 Great Britain
AD Warwick House Practice Association
DES Jack Gardner
better relationship between doctor and
patient, pour meilleures relations entre
docteur et clients, für besseres
Verständigung zwischen Arzten und
Patienten

5 Japan
AD World Crafts Council
AG Ikko Tanaka
DIR Ikko Tanaka
DES Ikko Tanaka/Tet Suya Oht

10 Yugoslavia
AD Dukat, Mljekara Zagreb
AG Apel
DIR/DES Zeljko Borčić
ILL Ivica Vidović
dairy products, produits laitiers,
Milchprodukte

11 Austria
AD Reise-Club 'Rheintal' Höchst
AG Vorarlberger Graphik
DIR/DES Othmar Motter
travel agency, agence de voyages,
Organisator von Gesellschaftsreisen

16 Japan
AD Zuzu Co Ltd
AG Kasugain Co Ltd
DIR Shozo Murase
DES Shigeyuki Hattori

17 Austria
AD Koloman Mandler
AG Badian & Weinblatt Visuelles Design
Studio
DIR/DES Joey Badian
ring books

12 Japan
AD Santomi Co Ltd
AG Kasugai Co Ltd
DIR Shozo Murase
DES Shigeyuki Hattori

18 Canada
AD Toronto General Hospital
AG Burns, Cooper, Hynes Ltd
DIR/DES Robert Burns
hospital

13 Hong Kong
AD PMP Advertising Ltd
DIR/DES Terence Yeung
CALLIGRAPHY Terrence Yeung
advertising agents

19 Great Britain
AD Sturla Holdings
AG Minale, Tattersfield & Ptnrs.
DES M. Minale/Brian Tattersfield
financing company, companie financière,
Finanzgesellschaft

14 Great Britain
AD Edinburgh International Festival
AG Forth Studios Ltd
DIR/DES John Martin
festival emblem

20 United States
AD Colorado State University
AG Mark Atkins Design
DIR/DES/ILL Mark Atkins
university

15 Austria
AD Exquisit Keramik Geist
AG Badian & Weinblatt Visuelles Design
Studio
DIR/DES Joey Badian
ceramics

**Trademarks
Marques
Schutzmarken**

1 Spain
AD Industria Linera SA
AG Art Top Diseno Grafico
DES Carlos Torres
textile industry

2 Holland
AD Druk en Papier
AG Brouwer Offset BV
DIR P. van Dijk
DES William Ebell
printing press

3 Bulgaria
AD Sofia Philharmonia
DES Stephan Kantscheff
orchestra

4 Italy
AD Ambra
AG Ferrante/Pollastrini
DES Carlo Pollastrini
cake decorations

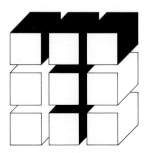

5 Australia
AD Trollope Graphics
AG Cato Hibberd Design Pty. Ltd
DIR/DES Ken Cato
display and exhibition designer, dessinateur
d'étalages et expositions

6 Brazil
AD Marli-Bras
AG Miran Estudio
DIR Oswaldo Miranda

7 Italy
AD Geoconsulting
AG Fantastics 4
DIR/DES Giovanni Lussu/Paola Trucco

8 Cuba
AD Dimano
AG Félix Beltrán
DIR/DES Félix Beltrán
sports centre, centre sportif

9 Germany
AD Olaf Gaumer Werbestudio
DIR/DES Olaf Gaumer
design studio

10 Norway
AD Resto Artists Materials
DES Hans Jørgen Toming
artist's materials

11 United States
AD Procter & Gamble
AG Lipson-Jacob Assoc.
DIR Sam Ross
DES Stan Brod
chemicals

12 Germany
Ad Arbeitsgruppe Traum und soziale
Wirklichkeit
AG Reflex
DIR/DES Feller
working party 'Dream and reality'

13 Japan
AD Isetan Department Store
AG Nippon Design Center
DIR/DES Kenzo Nakagawa
department store, magasin

14 Spain
AD Biblos
AG F. Bas
DIR/DES Francisco Bas
publishers

15 Germany
AD Walter Horn
DIR/DES Herbert Wenn
architect

16 Great Britain
AD Youth and Music
AG John Marsh Design
DIR/DES John Marsh

17 Ireland
AD European Patent Organisation
AG Kilkenny Design Workshops
DIR/DES/ILL Tony O'Hanlon

18
AD Kaj Harring AS
AG Niels Andersen Reklame
DIR ole Kragh-Sørensen Copy & Art Direction
DES Ole Kragh-Sørensen
lighting accessories, accessoires d'éclairage,
elektrische

19 United States
AD Triton College
AG Edward Hughes
DIR/DES Edward Hughes
Community College

20 Germany
AD Brandt Augenoptiker
DES Erich Unger
optician

1a-c Argentina
AD Sistema Tipo de Senalamiento Urbano y Edilicio
AG Arq. Gonzalez Ruiz y Asociados
DIR/DES Guillermo González Ruiz
sign system for Argentinian new towns under construction: a) Wild Life b) Flora c) folk objects
systéme d'embléms pour nouvelles villes en construction en Argentine: a) Faune b) Flore c) Folklore
Bildzeichen für neue Siedlungen, (a) Fauna, (b) Flora, (c) Volkskun

2a-c Great Britain
AD Diamond Stylus Company Ltd
AG Your Company by Design
DIR/DES Derrick Holmes
gramophone record cleaning equipment

3 Denmark
AD Interair
AG Niels Hartmánn
DES Flemming Nielsen
air company,

4a-b Israel
AD Koor Industries Ltd
AG Forum-Public Relations Studio Gal
DIR Shoshana Cohen
DES Yona Grinbaum
facts and figures,

1a
1b
1c

2a-c

5 Holland
AD N.V. Luchthaven Schiphol
AG NPO
DIR/DES Peter Wagner
housestyle Schiphol Airport

6 Spain
AD Fernando Medina Design
DIR/DES Fernando Medina
Alphaville

7 Germany
AD Deutsche Bank
AG/DES Stankowski & Partner
bank

8 Canada
AD Kent Allan Ltd
DIR Kenneth Seabrook
corporate identity for Equipment Rentals Ltd

3

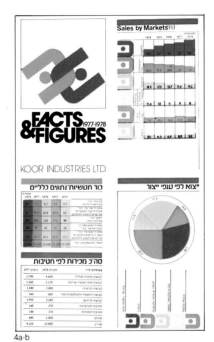

4a-b

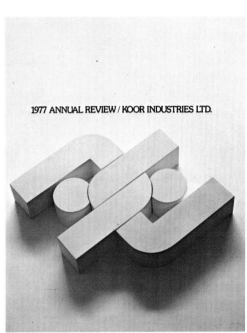

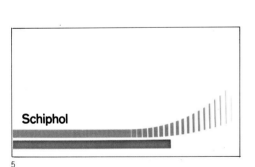

5

6

7

8

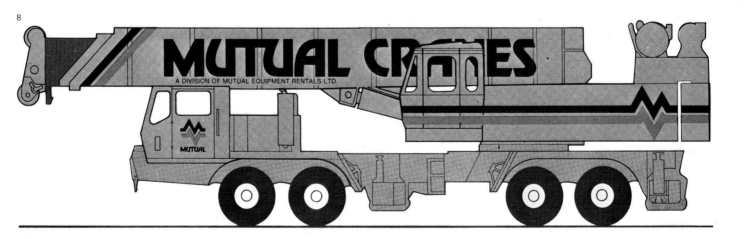

Letterheads
en têtes
Briefköpfe

1 Holland
AD Eduard Mlinar
DIR/DES Eduard Mlinar

2 United States
AD The Design Group Inc
AG Gauger Sparks Silva
DIR/DES Walter Sparks
ILL Paulette Traverso

3 Great Britain
AD Conran Associates
DIR/DES Stafford Cliff
Design studios

4 Great Britain
AD John Astrop
DES John Astrop
designer

5 Spain
AD Eix Arquitectura
AG Eix
DIR/DES Roberto Dosil
architects' group, groupe d'architectes

6 Canada
AD Paul Epp
AG Burns, Cooper, Hynes Ltd
DIR/DES Robert Burns

1

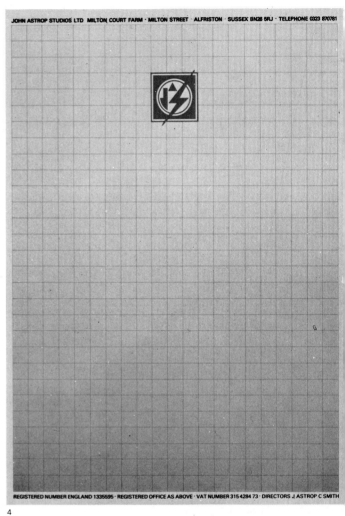

4

2

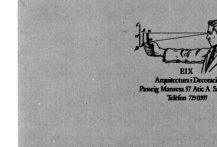

3

CONRAN ASSOCIATES
28 Neal Street, London WC2H 9PH. Telephone 01-240 3474. Telex 25701.

Paul Epp Designer/Woodworker 134 Cornell Street Cambridge Ontario N3H 1K4 Telephone (519) 653-8560

7 Great Britain
AD TUB Promotions
AG Bogdan Zarkowski
DIR/DES/ILL Bogdan Zarkowski

8 Mexico
AD Golf Editores SA
AG 8008 Diseno, SC (ocho mil ocho)
DIR Fernando Mariscal
DES Eugenia Trillas
ILL Ismael Salas
publishers

9 Italy
AD Giuliano Vittori
DES Giuliano Vittori

10 Great Britain
AD Prime Computer International
AG Bloy Eldridge
DIR Robert Custance
DES Helena Pessi-Wilkinson

11 Great Britain
AD Moo Movies
DES Ian Moo Young, Ginni Moo Young,
Roger Walton

12 Italy
AD Alphabetafilm
AG Giuliano Vittori
DES Giuliano Vittori

TUB
TUB Promotions
3 Okeover Manor, 23 Northside,
Clapham Common, London SW4
01-622 8396

Proprietor
M.J.T.Wainwright

7

PRIME COMPUTER **INTERNATIONAL**

Prime Computer International The Hounslow Centre Lampton Road Hounslow Middlesex TW3 1JB Telephone 01-572 6241 Telex 938371

10

8

Golf
Editores

Dr. Gustavo Baz 288 Tlanepantla, Edo. de México Tel. 397 8644

11

Ian Moo Young
MOO MOVIES
55 Neal Street
London WC2
01-836 7404

9

Giuliano Vittori
grafico
c/o ITER
via Giacomo Faffaelli 1
tel. (06) 557 4305 / 5578249
00146 Roma

12

ALPHABETAFILM
società per azioni
Sede legale e uffici
via Asiago 2
tel. (06) 383093 / 382907
00195 Roma

Letterheads
en têtes
Briefköpfe

1 Great Britain
AD A & M Records
AG David Tyrell & Associates
DIR Michael Ross
DES David Tyrell
ILL Adrian Chesterman
record company publicity department,

2 Italy
AG Guliano Vittori
DES Guliano Vittori
ILL Pablo Echaurren

3 South Africa
AD Pierre Hinch
AG Derek Spaull Graphics
DIR/DES Derek Spaull

4 Israel
AD Ouhaf/Karmon/Shifrin/Na'aman
AG Ouhaf/Karmon/Shifrin/Na'aman
DIR/DES Yak Milho
advertising agency

5 Great Britain
AD Peter Kerr Design Associates Ltd
AG Peter Kerr Design Associates Ltd
DIR/DES Peter Kerr
graphic/package/product design
dessin/emballage/maquette de produit
Verpackungsentwurf

6 United States
AD Joe Scorsone
DIR/DES/ILL Joe Scorsone
designer

1

2

3

Giuliano Vittori
disegno progettazione grafica

via degli Scipioni 237a
tel. (06) 353204
00192 Roma

4

5

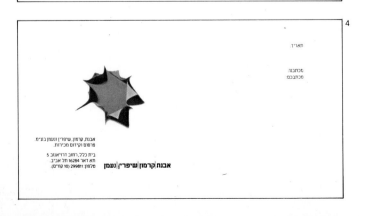

Peter Kerr Design Associates Ltd

11a Sidney Road
Walton-on-Thames
Surrey KT12 2NA
Walton-on-Thames 22483

Spanish office
Catalina de Erauso
20 (Amara)
San Sebastian
Spain
Telephone 010 3443 46 47 76

Graphic design
Package design
Product design

7 United States
AD Lanny Sommese Design
DIR/DES/ILL Lanny Sommese
design studio, studio

8 Spain
AD Fernando Medina
AG/DIR Fernando Medina
design studio

9 Great Britain
AD Tiger Securities
AG Minale Tattersfield and Partners
DIR/DES M. Minale, Brian Tattersfield,
Nick Wurr
letterhead for Tiger Sports

10 Hong Kong
AD Yokohama Import & Export Co
AG Alpha Advertising Ltd
DIR/DES Louis Ching-Ho Wong

11 Australia
AD Pope & Kiernan and Black Advertising
STUDIO Graphic Concept
DIR Ray Black
DES/ILL Maurice Schlesinger

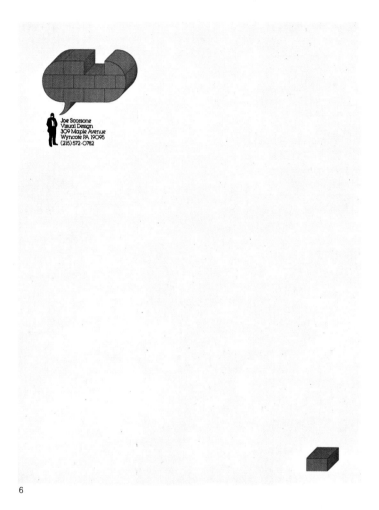

6

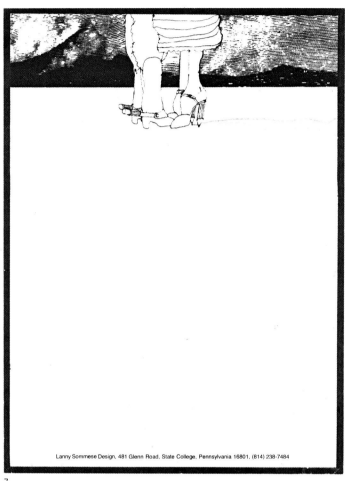

Lanny Sommese Design, 481 Glenn Road, State College, Pennsylvania 16801, (814) 238-7484

7

Fernando Medina Diseño

8

TIGER SPORTS
A member of the Tiger Securities Group

9

10

11

**Letterheads
en têtes
Briefköpfe**

1 Brazil
AD Miran Estudio
DIR/DES Oswaldo Miranda (Miran)

2 Great Britain
AD Walker Pannell Presentations
DES Ethan Ames
threatrical producers, producteurs de théatre

3 Germany
AD Dr. Günther Scholtz
DIR/DES/ILL Herbert Wenn
dentist, dentiste

4 Great Britain
AD El Golfo Golf Club
AG Howe Design
DIR/DES Joe Howe

5 Great Britain
AD Roy Adams MTPI
DES Alan G. Livingston
town and country planner, depinateur ville et
campagne, Stadtplanung

6 United States
AD The New Company
AG The Marketing Department
DIR/DES Bob Coonts

1

4

5

2

6

3

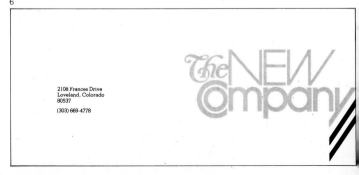

7 Germany
AD Iris Schirp
DIR/DES Herbert Wenn
gymnastics for sick people, gymnastique
pour malades, Sport für Körperlich

8 Great Britain
AD City Business Careers
AG Moo Movies
DIR/DES Roger Walton
accountants recruitment agency
agence d'emploi pour comptables,
Anstellungsrermittlung für Buchhalter

9 Spain
AD Indar
DIR/DES Salvatore Adduci

10 Great Britain
AD Nature Conservancy Council
AG Conran Associates
DIR/DES Paul Clarke
ILL Jane Hibbert

11 Great Britain
AD Chorel Music
AG Wide Art Studios
DIR/DES/ILL James Hutcheson
'jingle' firm, Musikagentur

12 Great Britain
AD Liberty & Co Ltd
AG Derek Forsyth Partnership
DIR/DES Michael Staniford
department store, magasin, Warenhaus

7

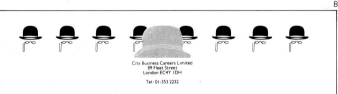

8

10

11

12

Packaging
Emballages
Verpackungsgestaltung

1 Great Britain
AD A & M Records Ltd
STUDIO A & M Records Ltd
DIR Michael Ross
DES/ILL John Cokell and Stephen Lavers
promotion of record by 'the Tubes',
promotion d'un disque

2a-b Australia
AD Heinemann Educational Australia
DIR David Deakin
DES/ILL David Deakin
boxes containing project material for a social
science scheme, boites contenant le matériel
pour un projet de sociologie, Lehrmaterial

3 Great Britain
AD Michael Barrie
STUDIO Michael Peters & Partners Ltd
DIR Michael Peters
DES Madeleine Bennett
carrier bags for chain of menswear shops,
sacs pour une chaine de boutiques pour
hommes, Tragbeutel für Modegeshäfte

2a

2b

3

Packaging
Emballages
Verpackungsgestaltung

1 Australia
AD Tucker & Kidd
AG Tucker & Kidd
DIR/DES Barrie Tucker
ILL Robert Marshall
design studio's Christmas gift to clients,
projet pour cadeaux de Noël aux clients d'un
studio

2 South Africa
AD 6th Sense Beechams SA
AG A.D.A.M. (pty.) ltd
DIR/DES Clive Gay

3 Canada
AD Canada Packers Ltd
DES Stewart & Morrison Ltd
frozen dairy dessert,

4 Hong Kong
AD Holiday Inn Hong Kong
AG Holiday Inn International Asia/Pacific In-
house Advertising Agency
DIR William W.K. Liu
DES Tommy Dy
hotel

5 Canada
AD Yardley of London (Canada) Ltd
AG Burns, Cooper, Hynes Ltd
DIR/DES Robert Burns, Heather Cooper
packaging for range of cosmetics, emballage
pour cosmétiques

6 United States
AD Honeywell Inc
DIR/DES Cyril John Schlosser
computers

1

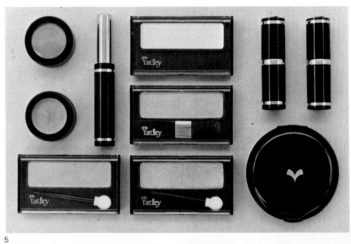

2

3

4

6

5

7   8

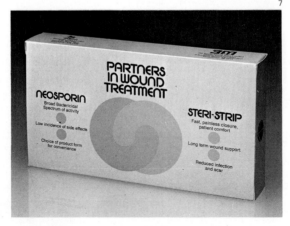

7 South Africa
AD Wellcome (Pty.) Ltd
AG Derek Spaull Graphics
DIR/DES Derek Spaull
pharmaceuticals

8 South Africa
AD Parke-Davis
AG Derek Spaull Graphics
DIR/DES Derek Spaull
pharmaceuticals

9 Great Britain
AD Dema Glass Ltd
AG David Harris Consultant Design
DIR/DES David Harris
ILL FNG Clarke Ltd
gift pack for Chateau drinking glasses,
emballage cadeau pour verres à vin

10 Denmark
AD F.D.P.
AG R.T.
DES Nina Benko Lassen
wine labels, étiquettes pour vins

11a-b Canada
AD Yardley of London (Canada) Ltd
AG Burns, Cooper, Hynes Ltd
DIR Robert Burns, Heather Cooper
DES Heather Cooper, Carmen Dunjko
soaps, emballage pour savons

9

10

11a

11b

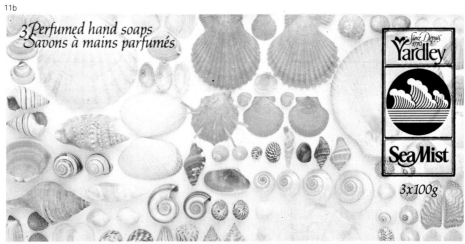

Packaging
Emballages
Verpackungsgestaltung

1 Brazil
AD Cantâo 4
AG Dia Design Ltda
DIR Renato Gomes/Gilberto Strunck
ILL Roberta Rocha
carrier bags, boxes, sacs d'emballages,
boîtes

2 India
AD Air-India
STUDIO Air-India Art Studio
DIR J.B. Cowasji
DES R.M. Kharat
ILL S.A. Gupte
shopping bag, sac à provisions

3 Great Britain
AD Scottish Fine Soaps Ltd
AG Russell Design Associates
DIR/DES Evelyn P. Russell
ILL Maggie Wallace
soap packaging, emballage de savon

4 Germany
AD Parker
AG Naghi Naghachian
pre-school toys

5 Great Britain
AD Penhaligon's
AG Michael Peters & Partners Ltd
DIR Michael Peters
DES Madeleine Bennett
cosmetics

6 Austria
AD Schüller & Co AG
AG Badian & Weinblatt Visuelles Design
Studio
DIR/DES Joey Badian
price tags

1

2

3

4

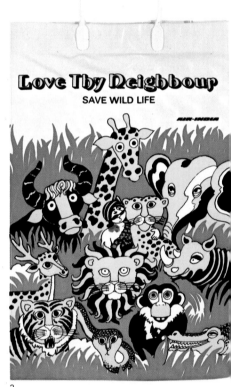

5

7 South Africa
AD Warner
AG Derek Spaull Graphics
DIR/DES Derek Spaull
sample pack for orange flavoured cough
linctus, sinutoss and bottle of cointreau

8 United States
AD Pepsico Wines and Spirits
AG Pepsi-Cola Graphic Arts Dept.
DIR Frank Rupp
DES Sandra Schoultz
ILL Dennis Lyle
bottle and label design for line of Japanese
wines

9 South Africa
AD Reckitt Toiletries
AG Reckitt and Coleman Packaging and
Promotion Dept.
DIR David Neville
DES Michael Edwards
ILL Michael Edwards
spray deodorants, déodorisants

10 Great Britain
AD Pearsons of Chesterfield
AD Ad Graphics Ltd
DIR/DES Brian Davis
ILL Bernard Chandler
traditional stoneware, poterie de grès,
Tonwaren

6

7

8

9

10

Packaging
Emballages
Verpackungsgestaltung

1 Denmark
AD Jydsk Kløver Maelk
AG Marketing Nord
DIR/DES Henning Aardstrup
packaging for yoghurt, emballage pour yaourt

2 Canada
AD British Columbia Liquor Distribution
AG Kent Allan Ltd
DIR Kent Allan
DES Kenneth Seabrook

3 Great Britain
AD Marks & Spencer
AG Marks & Spencer
DIR Ken Jones/Charles Wilkinson
DES Charles Wilkinson
box for frozen pizzas

4 Denmark
AD ASIK (Hospital Supplies) Denmark
AG Eric Alsing Reklame
DIR/DES Erik Alsing
disposable syringes,

5 Germany
AD Bäderland GmbH
AG HDA International
DES Klaus Schmidt/C.H. Tay
bathroom equipment, boutique de fourniture
de salles de bain, Badezimmerartikel

6 Great Britain
AD Barrs Soft Drinks
AG Howe Design
DIR/DES Joe Howe
Tizer box

1

2

3

4

5

6

7

8

7 New Zealand
AD Industrial Chm. Ind. Ltd
AG Design Link Ltd
DIR P.E. Burke
DES David Backhurst
packaging for industrial and retail degreaser
agent, emballage pour agence de
degraissement industrielle et retail

8 South Africa
AD Reckitt Toiletries
AG Packaging & Promotion Dept. Reckitt &
Colman
DIR David Neville
DES/ILL Michael Edwards
deodorant for men, déodorisant pour
hommes

9 Great Britain
AD Johnson & Johnson
AG Michael Peters & Partners Ltd
DIR Michael Peters
DES Howard Milton
bottle and package design for a range of skin
care products

10 Hong Kong
AD Dymo (Hong Kong) Ltd
AG Tse-Needham Advertising International
Ltd
DIR/DES/ILL Raymond Chan
packaging design for Dymo tapewriter for
children

11 Japan
AD Earth Chemical, Ako-city
AG Nippon International Agency
DIR/DES Helmut Schmid
Hi-Earth insecticide

12 South Africa
AD Royal Baking Powder SA
AG A.D.A.M. (Pty.) Ltd
DIR/DES Clive Gay
hot sponge pudding

13 Belgium
AD Pic-Nic
DES Robert Valck
PHOTO Hug Bal

14 Germany
AD Heinz Loeser Wohnbedarf
AG Zisowsky & Oehring
DIR/DES Zisowsky & Oehring

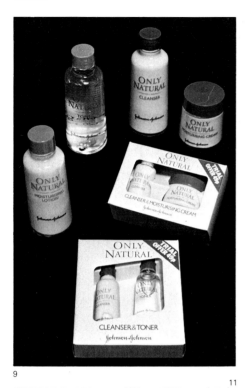

9

10

11

12

13

14

Packaging
Emballages
Verpackungsgestaltung

1 Great Britain
AD Phonogram Ltd
AG Hothouse
DIR Alan Schmidt
ILL Geoff Halpin

2 Germany
AD Ariola-Eurodisc GmbH
AG Ariola-Eurodisc GmbH
DIR/DES Manfred Vormstein
ILL Manfred Vormstein

3 Great Britain
AD A & M Records Ltd
AG A & M Records Ltd
DIR Michael Ross and Ethan A. Russell
DES Nick Marshall, Michael Ross and Ethan
A. Russell
PHOTO Ethan A. Russell

4 Great Britain
AD MCA Records
AG Cream

5 Great Britain
AD Bruce Findlay-Zoom Records
AG Wide Art Studios
DIR/DES/ILL James Hutcheson

1

2

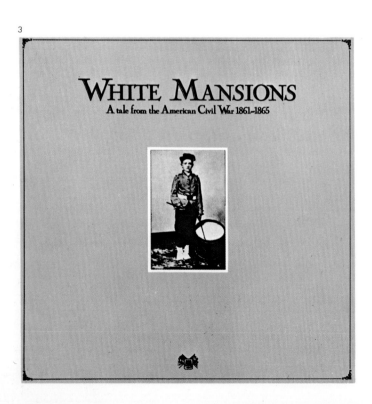

3

4

6a-b Israel
AD CBS Records
AG David Tartakover
DIR/DES David Tartakover
ILL (a) Avi Ganor (b) Gerard Alon

7 Great Britain
AD CBS Records
AG Wide Art Studios
DIR Roslav Szaybo
DES James Hutcheson
PHOTO Victor Albrow

5

6a

6b

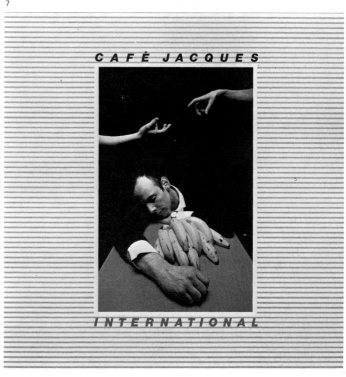

7

Packaging
Emballages
Verpackungsgestaltung

1 South Africa
AD Reckitt Hardware
AG Package & Promotion Dept. Reckitt & Colman
DIR David Neville
DES/ILL Malcolm W. Bates
timber floor treatments,

2 Denmark
AD F.D.B.
AG RT
DES Nina Benko Lassen
underwear, sousvêtements, Unterwäsche

3 Germany
AD Schuh-Union-AG
AG Olaf Gaumer
DIR/DES Olaf Gaumer
shoes, chaussures Schuhe

4 Denmark
AD F.D.B.
AG R.T.
DES Peter Abelin
pancake flour, farine pour crêpes,
Pfannkuchenmehl

5 South Africa
AD Propart Sigma Motor Corporation
AG A.D.A.M. (Pty.) Ltd
DIR/DES Clive Gay/Mr Allen

6 Great Britain
AD Esso Petroleum Co Ltd
AG Cato Johnson Ltd
DIR Dick O'Brien
DES Richard Tilley/Sue Malin
packaging for motor oil, emballage pour huile de moteur, Motorenöl

1

2

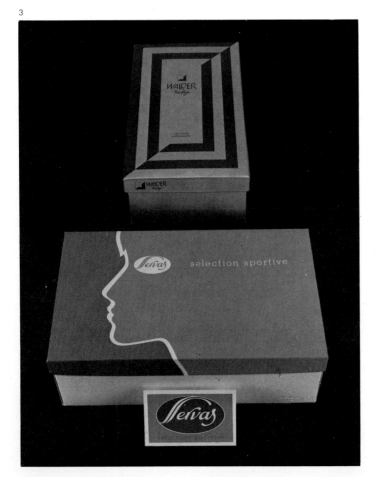

3

4

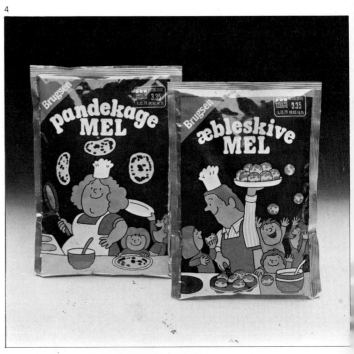

7 South Africa
AD Reckitt Household Products
AG Packaging & Promotion Dept. Reckitt &
Colman
DIR David Neville
DES Fred Weidmann
ILL Ellaphie Ward
air freshener, purificateur pour air

8 Denmark
AD F.D.B.
AG R.T.
DES Per Jørgensen
shaving foam, mousse à raser, Rasierschaum

9 Great Britain
AD The Yellow Can Company
STUDIO Michael Peters & Partners Ltd
DIR Michael Peters
DES Bev Whitehead
aerosol cans, bombes aérosol

10 Italy
AD Dibiten
AG Ferrante/Pollastrini
DES Carlo Pollastrini
paint pots

5

6

7

8

9

10

Packaging
Emballages
Verpackungsgestaltung

1 Australia
AD Berri Estates Winery
STUDIO Tucker & Kidd
DIR Ian Kidd
DES Ian Kidd/Barrie Tucker
ILL Robert Marshall
special pack of 6 award-winning red wines,
boite spéciale pour six vins ayant reçu un prix

2 Brazil
AD Niccolini
AG/DIR/DES Fred Jordan
promotion for printing on aluminium foil,
promotion pour impression sur papier
aluminium

3 Australia
AD Honeytree Vineyard
AG Graphic Concept
DIR Maurice Schlesinger
DES/ILL Maurice Schlesinger
wine labels, étiquettes pour vins

4 Great Britain
AD Wiggins Teape (Toys and Crafts) Ltd
AG Ad Graphics Ltd
DIR/DES Brian Davis
ILL David Lawson
packs for games, emballages pour jeux

5 Great Britain
AD Interpharma Distributing Co
DES Richard Ward
COPY Ian Kidd
shampoo

6a-b Germany
AD FA Wispi
AG FA Illert GmbH
DES Karl Heinz Franck
COPY Fa. Illert GmbH

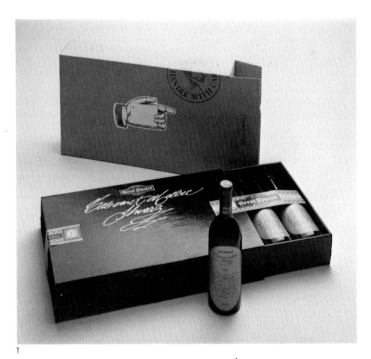

1

2

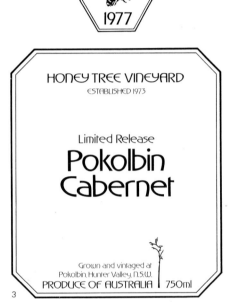

3

4

5

6a

7

8

6b

7 Denmark
AG R.T.
DES Jørgen Madsen
hamburgers

8 Spain
AD Pervisa SA
AG Carlos Torres Diseno Grafico
DES Carlos Torees
bath and shower gel
gelée pour bain et douche

9a-c Great Britain
AD Listen for Pleasure
AG MFP Design Studio
DIR/DES David Wharin
ILL (a) Margaret Tempest (c) Michael Lye
casette book cover, couverture et emballage
pour livres casettes

10 Great Britain
AD Penhaligon
AG Michael Peters & Partners Ltd
DIR Michael Peters
cosmetics

11 Greece
AD D. Kourtakis AE
AG K & K Unicas Advertising Centre
DIR/DES Yiannis Angelopoulos
ILL Patrice van Puyvelde
retsina wine, vin résiné

12 Canada
AD Rieder Distillery Ltd
AG Raymond Lee and Associates Ltd
DIR/DES Raymond Lee
brandy

13 Germany
AD Mario Pellarin
DIR Herbert Wenn
guitar strings, cordes de guitare, Guitairen
saiten

132-133

9a-c

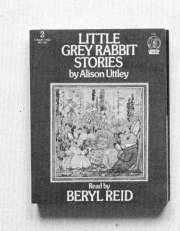

10

11

12

13

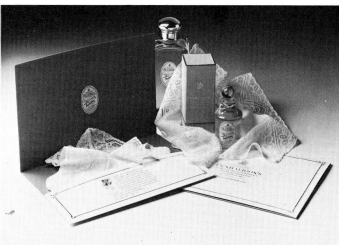

**Packaging
Emballages
Verpackungsgestaltung**

1a-d Malaysia
AD Zaza Boutique
AG KHK Creative Communications
DIR/DES Kolt Hong Kong
boutiques selling clothes and accessories,
boutique de vêtements et accessoires

2 Australia
AD Robert Timms Pty Ltd
AG Cato Hibberd Design Pty. Ltd
packaging and catering pack of instant coffee,
emballage de café soluble pour restaurants

3 Denmark
AD F.D.B.
AG R.T.
DES Nina Benko Lassen
roll-on deodorant, déodorisant sur rouleau

4 Brazil
AD Cantao 4
AG Dia Design Ltda
DIR/DES Renato Gomes/Gilberto Strunck
ILL Roberto Rocha
labels, étiquettes

5 Argentina
AD Via Valrossa
AG Estudio Jorge Canale
DIR Jorge Canale

6 Australia
AD National Chemical Products Pty Ltd
AG Cato Hibberd Design Pty Ltd
DIR Ken Cato
DES/ILL Cato Hibberd Design Pty Ltd
hair shampoo/lightener,

1a

1b

1c

1d

2

3

4a-f

7 Belgium
AD Oubry
DES Robert Valck
PHOTO Hug-Bal
flour, farine, Mehl

8 Spain
AD Reira Marsa
AG Publicidad Mediterranea
DIR Ramiro Seguna
DES Enrique Fernandez
ILL Enuase Nata
dessert

9 South Africa
AD Warner
AG Derek Spaull Graphics
DIR/DES Derek Spaull

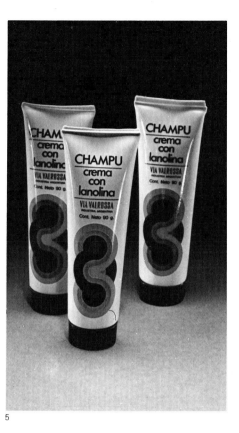

5

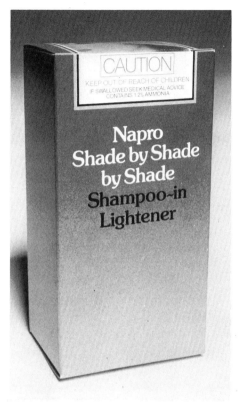

6

7

8 9

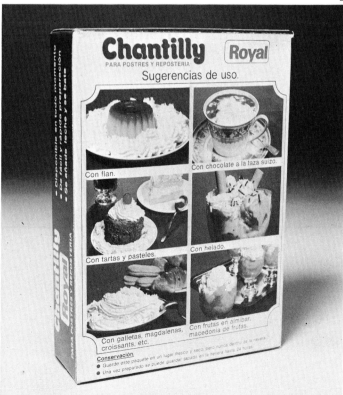

1 Spain
AD Saflor SA
AG Esege SA
DIR/DES Miguel A. Zapata Garcia

2 Denmark
AD F.D.B.
AG RT
DIR Jørgen Madsen
DES Hanne Andersen
soft drinks, boissons non-alcoholisées,
alkoholfreie betränke

3 Spain
AD Monerris Planelles
AG Asterisco
DIR/DES Salvatore Adduci
nougat

4 Canada
AD Chocolate Fantasies
AG Burns, Cooper, Hynes Ltd
DIR Robert Burns
DES/ILL Roxanne Mitchell
chocolate

5 Mexico
AD Productos Alianza
AG Unidad Diseno SC
DIR Arq. Mario Lazo
DES Jorge Canales

6 Argentina
AD Cannon SACI
DIR/DES/ILL Jorge Daniel Soler
toiletries for children, accessoires de toilette
pour enfants, Toilettenartikel für Kinder

1

2

3

4

5

7 Great Britain
AD Seagrams UK Ltd
AG Michael Peters & Partners Ltd
DIR Michael Peters
DES Madeleine Bennett
scotch whisky

8a-c Great Britain
AD The Ravenhead Company Ltd
AG Ad Graphics Ltd
DIR (A, c) Ken Brown (b) Brian Davis
DES Brian Davis
ILL (a) David Lawson (b) Brian Davis
    (c) David Lawson
range of table glass,

6

7

8a

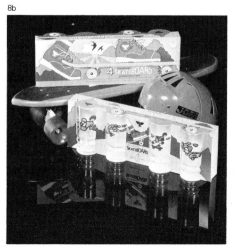

8b

8c

Screen advertising
Titles
Annonces de l'écran
Titres
Film und TV Werbung
Titel

1a-h Great Britain
AD Thames TV
DIR/DES Bernard Allum
ILL Roy Knipe
titles for documentary on the Russian revolution

2 Great Britain
AD Granada T.V. Manchester
DES Donald Stevens
main title lettering for drama series

3 Bulgaria
AD Nikola Petrov Nikolov
AG Bulgarian Television
DES Nikola Petrov Nikolov
60th anniversary of the Soviet State, le 60ème anniversaire de l'état sovietique, 60 jahrestag der russischen Revolution

4 Italy
AD Rai—Radiotelevisione Italiana
AG Ruffolo—Studio Grafico
DIR/DES Sergio Ruffolo
pages from History

1a-h

2

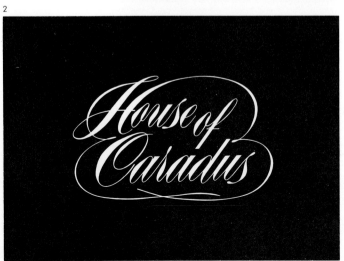

3

5a-b United States
AD Jovan Inc Chicago
AG J. Walter Thompson, Chicago
DIR Mary Aries
DES Richard Williams
perfume

6a-c Great Britain
AD Granada T.V. Manchester
DES Donald Stevens
TV station weather slides
planches météorologique pour station de
télévision, Wetterbericht

4

5a

5b

6a

6b

6c

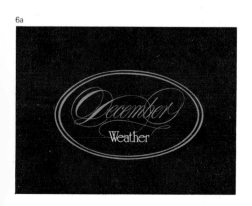

Screen advertising
Titles
Annonces de l'écran
Titres
Film und TV Werbung
Titel

1 Italy
AD RAI—Radiotelevisione Italiana
AG Ruffolo—Studio Graffico
DIR/DES Sergio Ruffolo

2 Germany
AD Zweites Deutsches Fernsehen
AG Christof Gassner Grafik-Design
DES Christof Gassner

3a-c Italy
AD Radiotelevisione Italiana
AG Studio de Santis
DIR/DES Alfredo de Santis
titles

4a-d Holland
AD Het Nederlands Zuivelbureau
AG Prad BV
DIR Huib Ebbinge
campaign for milk, campagne pour le lait

5 Germany
AD Zweites Deutsches Fernsehen
AG Christof Gassner Grafik-Design
DES Christof Gassner
TV drama, théatre à la télévision

 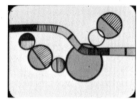  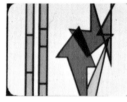 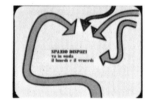

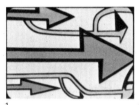    

1

2

3a

3b

3c
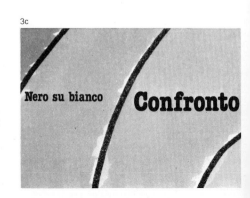

4a

4b

4c

4d

5

Screen advertising
Titles
Annonces de l'écran
Titres
Film und TV Werbung
Titel

1a-d Holland
AD Seven-Up Nederland
AG Prad BV
DIR Joop Smit/Jolle Westermann
DES Theo Strengers
ILL Tony Cattaneo
soft drink, boissons non alcooholisées,
limonade

2 Great Britain
AD K-Tel International UK Ltd
AG Hedley Griffin Films
DIR Ian Duncan
DES/ILL Hedley Griffin
record commercial, publicité pour disque,
Schallplatten

3 Italy
AD Radiotelevisione Italiana
AG Studio de Santis
DIR/DES Alfredo de Santis
open school, program educatif,
Erzehungsprogramm

4a-f Brazil
AD Rede Globo TV
DIR/DES Rudi Böhm
première '78

5a-f Brazil
AD Rede Globe TV
AG TV Globo (I.F. Studios)
DIR/DES Rudi Böhm
TV station sign, station de télévision

1a

1b

1c

1d

2

3

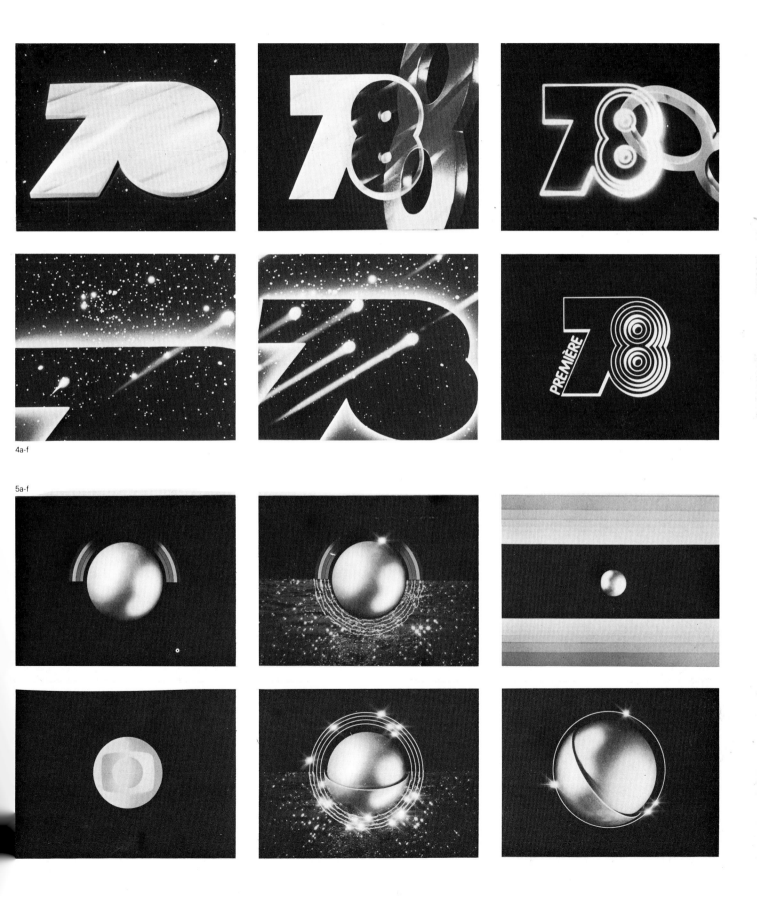

4a-f

5a-f

Screen advertising
Titles
Annonces de l'écran
Titres
Film und TV Werbung
Titel

1a-e Israel
AD Israel TV Network
DIR/DES Benny Levine
news, nouvelles, Nachrichten

2 Great Britain
AD Granada TV Manchester
DES Donald Stevens
logo for documentary series,

3 Bulgaria
AD Bulgarian TV
AG Nikola Petrov Nikolov
DES Nikola Petrov Nikolov
'science and technical progress', progrés
dans la science et la technique

4 Germany
AD Zweites Deutsches Fernsehen
AG Christof Gassner Grafik-Design
DES Christof Gassner
'Shakespeare cycle',

5a-d Belgium
AD Banque Populaire et Crédit Mutuel
AG J. Walter Thompson, Brussels
PROD Wyatt Cattaneo Studios
DIR Ron Wyatt/Chris Randall
DES Beth McFall

6a-b Great Britain
AD Access
AG Geers Gross Advertising
PROD Wyatt Cattaneo Studios
DIR/DES Wyatt Cattaneo
credit cards

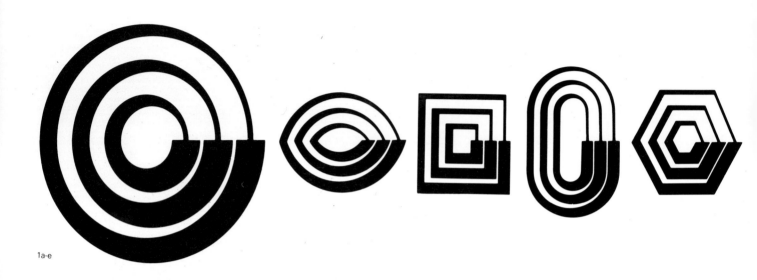

1a-e

2

3

4

7a-c Great Britain
AD Country Life English Butter
AG Geers Gross Advertising
PROD Wyatt Cattaneo Studio
DIR Ramón Modiano
DES Tony Cattaneo
butter, beurre

8a-c Switzerland
AD Schweizerischer Bankverein
AG Adolf Wirz AG
PROD Wyatt Cattaneo Studios
DIR Alison de Vere
DES Ellis Nadler
ANIM John Offord

5a

5b

5c

5d

6a-b

7a

7b

7c

8a

8b

8c

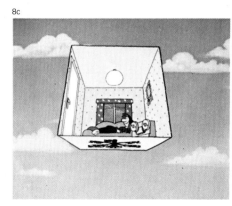

Screen advertising
Titles
Annonces de l'écran
Titres
Film und TV Werbung
Titel

1a-f Holland
AD House Painters Trade Organizations
AG NPO/Nationale Publiciteits Onderneming
DIR Herman Gerritzen
DES/ILL Max Velthuijs
indoor painting during wintertime, décoration
intérieure pendant l'hiver, Innendekoration im
Winter

2a-j Italy
AD RAI-Radiotelevisione Italiana
AG Ruffolo—Studio Grafino
DIR/DES Sergio Ruffolo

3a-c Brazil
AD Rede Globo
AG TV Globo
DIR/DES Rudi Böhm
World Cup

4a-d France
AD Crédit Lyonnais
AG Intermarco—Paris
DIR/DES Tony Cattaneo

5a-c Great Britain
AD Granada Television
AG Granada Studios
ILL Anna Farrar
children's programme

1a-f

2a-j

3a-c

4a

4b

4c

4d

5a

5b

5c

Screen advertising
Titles
Annonces de l'écran
Titres
Film und TV Werbung
Titel

1 Great Britain
AD Thames Television
DIR/DES Ethan Ames
current affairs, actualitées

2a-f Great Britain
AD Granada Television
AG Granada TV Graphic Design Dept.
DIR/DES/ILL Murray Cook
'pop' music show, musique 'pop'

3a-f Brazil
AD Rede Globo
AG TV Globo
DIR/DES Rudi Böhm
World Cup, coupe mondiale

1

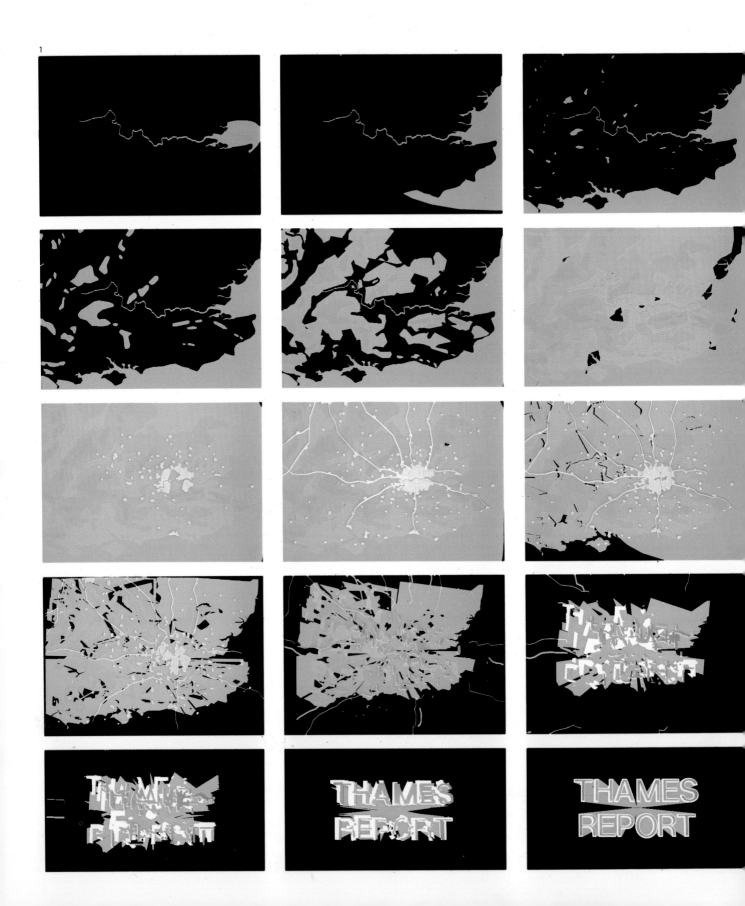

2a-f

3a-f

Screen advertising
Titles
Annonces de l'écran
Titres
Film und TV Werbung
Titel

1a-f Holland
AD Douwe Egberts Nederland
AG Prad BV
DIR Theo Strengers
coffee

2a-c Great Britain
AD Wyatt Cattaneo
DIR/DES Alison de Vere
entertainment film, film de divertissement

3a-d Great Britain
AD Sealink
AG AMB
PROD Wyatt Cattaneo Studios
DIR Chris Randall
DES Ron Wyatt
travel service, service de voyage, Reisebüro

1a-f

2a-c

3a-d

Direct Mail
Brochures
Broschüren

1-a-b Sweden
AD Plannja AB
AG Anderson & Lemble Vintergatan AB
DIR Bengt Johansson
DES Michel Roura
ILL Juiliano Sannicollo/Ingmar Halmasen
COPY Roger Ost/Bengt Johansson
range of new shades for roofing panels

1c-d Sweden
AD ASG AB
AG Anderson & Lembke Vintergatan AB
DIR Frank Gabriele
DES Erik Grönlund
ILL Bo Hylén
COPY Steve Trygg

1e-f Sweden
AD Swedforest Consulting
AG Anderson & Lembke Vintergatan AB
DIR Frank Gabriele
DES Erik Grönlund
ILL Photo agencies
COPY Tommie Afzelius
forestry consulting services

1g-h Sweden
AD Stalvaggar Pa Kontor
AG Anderson & Lembke Vintergatan AB
DIR Frank Gabriele
DES Erik Grönlund
office equipment

1i-j Sweden
AD SRA, Svenska Radio AB
AG Anderson & Lembke Vintergatan AB
DIR Frank Gabriele
DES Erik Grönlund
ILL Lasse Lie

DILEMMAT NÄR MAN SKA BESTÄMMA FÄRG PÅ HUS.

1a

1b

1c

1d

1e

1f

MELLANVÄGGAR I STÅL SOM DU ALDRIG SETT DEM.

1g

STÅLVÄGGAR PÅ KONTOR, IV.

1h

1i

1j

1 Great Britain
AD G & J Greenall Ltd
AG Royle Murgatroyd Design Associates Ltd
DIR Keith Murgatroyd
LETTER FORMS Tony Forster
price list brochure, livret liste des prix

2a-d Great Britain
AD (a-b) Wiggins Teape Ltd
   (c-d) Sealink, British Rail
AG Annual Reports Ltd
DIR Michael Peters
DES (a, b) Ben Whitehead
   (c, d) Jim Groark
ILL (a) Liz Moyes,
   (b) John Ireland
company reports

3a-c Great Britain
AD Baccarat
AG Negus & Negus
DIR Dick Negus
DES Dominic Negus
fashion show, spectrale de mode,

4a-d Great Britain
AD Gaff Management/Rod Stewart
AG Top Billing Publications Ltd
DIR/DES Bogdan Zarkowski
COPY John Pidgeon
souvenir brochure, livret souvenir

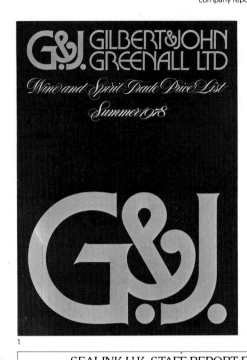

1

2a-b

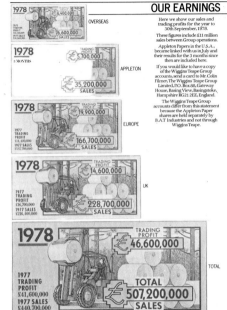

3

2c

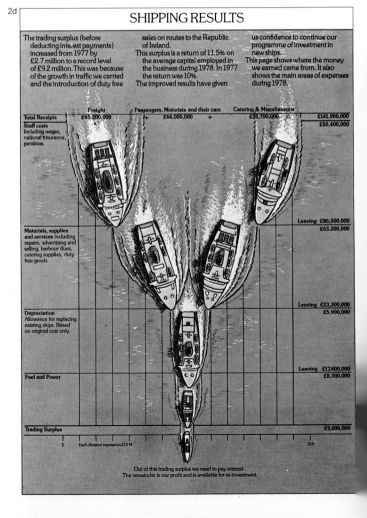

2d

3a

3b

3c

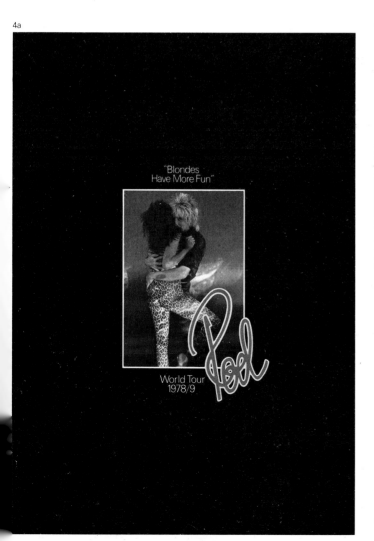

4a

CONTENTS

4b

1

INTRODUCTION

4c

ROD STEWART

3

4d

THE WATER

44

"Blondes
Have More Fun"

World Tour
1978/9

**Direct Mail
Brochures
Broschüren**

1a United States
AD I. Magnin
DIR Vicki Fischetti, Henry Wolf
DES Vicki Fischetti
ILL Henry Wolf
fashion, mode

1b United States
AD B.F. Goodrich
DIR Henry Wolf
DES David Blumenthal
ILL Nicholas Gaetano

2 Germany
AD/COPY Delden Gruppe
DES/ILL Barbara Buchwald
textiles

3 Canada
AD Yardley of London (Canada) Ltd
AG Burns, Cooper, Hynes Ltd
DIR Robert Burns
DES Dawn Cooper Tennant
ILL Book: Jeremiah Chechik, Product: Tim
Saunders
COPY Jim Hynes
cosmetics, cosmétiques

4 Germany
AD Bayerischer Rundfunk
DES Walter Tafelmaier
radio programmes

5 Canada
AD Catours (Eastern) Inc
AG Reinhold Schieber Assoc.
DIR/DES Reinhold Schieber
ILL Dave Clark
tourism

1a

1b

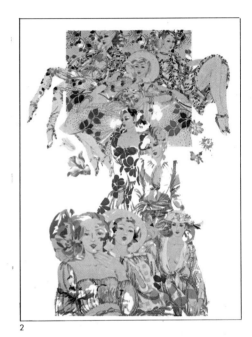

2

3

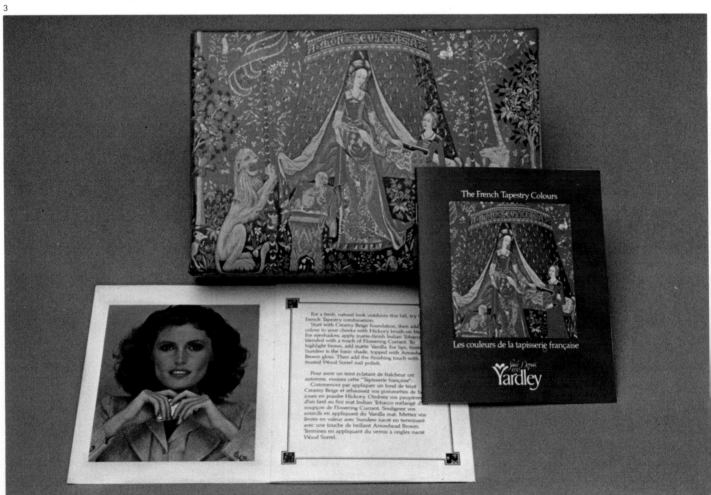

6 Holland
AD KIJK Magazine
AG KIJK Studio
DIR Peter van Leersum
DES Johan Ekkel
KIJK Magazine

7 Greece
AD Perlus Cruises Co Ltd
AG Elma Tsarouchi-Antoniadis
DIR/DES Elma Tsarouchi-Antoniadis
ILL Costis Antoniadis
COPY Elma Tsarouchi-Antoniadis

8 Great Britain
AD Smith Kline & French
AG Smith Kline & French Promotion Dept.
DIR A.G. Jones
ILL Paul Simmons
COPY I.S. Shires
Pharmaceuticals

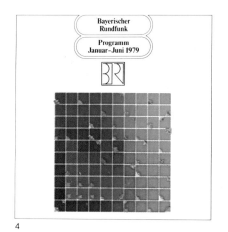

4

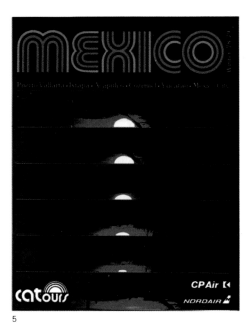

5

6

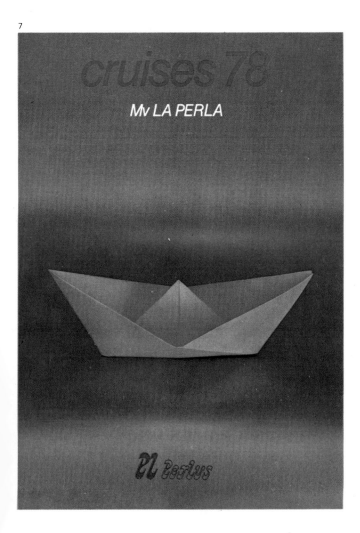

7

8

1a-b Holland
AD Sikkens
AG Conran Associates
DIR Paul Clarke/Gavin Clive-Smith
DES Stafford Cliff/Paul Clarke
ILL Kit Thomson/David Watson
COPY Derek Rourke
Decorette catalogue

1c France
AD Crayonne
AG Conran Associates
DIR Stafford Cliff
DES Paul Clarke/Sammy Farrington
COPY Peter Dixon
Crayonne products catalogue

2a-b Australia
AD Glover Gibbs
AG Tucker & Kidd
DIR Ian Kidd, Barrie Tucker
DES Ian Kidd
ILL Bernard Van Elsen/Stephen Graham
COPY Ian Kidd
pastrycooks and cake manufacturers,
Boulangers et patissiers, Bäckerei

3 Great Britain
AD CAP-CPP Ltd
AG Butler Cornfield Dedman Ltd
DIR/DES Paul Butler
ILL J. Wolstenholme
leaflet for computer trains at children's
computing exhibition, livret pour trains
computer à une exposition pour enfants

4 Great Britain
AD Yardley
AG Brick Studio Ltd
DIR Brian Plews
DES Geoff Ball
cosmetics

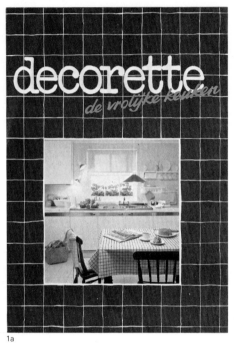

1a

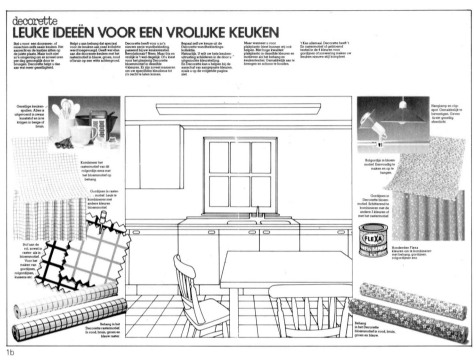

decorette
LEUKE IDEEËN VOOR EEN VROLIJKE KEUKEN

1b

1c

Kitchen shelves
Etagères de cuisine
Mensole per cucina
Küchenregale

A comprehensive and complementary range of four kitchen shelves in strong attractive thermoplastic:
shelf and hooks, shelf and sink tidy, shelf and kitchen roll holder, shelf and towel rails.

Série complète et complémentaire de quatre étagères de cuisine en thermoplastique solide et attrayant:
étagères à crochets, étagère et range-tour pour évier, étagère et porte-rouleau, étagère et rails pour serviettes.

Una gamma estesa e complementare di quattro mensole per cucina di materiale termoplastico robusto ed attraente:
mensola e ganci, mensola e contenitore, mensola e portacarta da cucina, mensola e stante porta asciugamani.

Eine vollständige und erganzende Linie, bestehend aus vier Küchenregalen in starkem attraktivem thermoplastischem
Material: Regal und Haken, Regal und Einsatz für die Spüle, Regal und Küchenrollenhalter, Regal und Handtuchscheren.

2a

2b

3

Welcome to the University of Newcastle-upon-Tyne Computing Laboratory Microcomputer Controlled Railway

Up to eight engines can be entirely controlled by a microcomputer. Indeed there is no other way to run them. If you want to have a go then you have to instruct the computer, and the computer will obey your commands.

Why?

Because it's fun
And because it is a good way to learn about microcomputers and programming, and about electronics. The current layout was designed, built and programmed by students as a necessary practical part of their training.

The team in charge of the layout at the moment wanted to run several engines at once. And they wanted them to run as fast as possible. But they agreed that collisions were expensive and must be avoided at all costs. They tried to do it with human operators and the results were disastrous.

How do you make it go?

Each engine on the track has a list of commands in the memory of the computer, for example:-

Start between NE and SU (Newcastle and Sunderland) moving towards Sunderland

speed 2 (go to Felixstowe)/speed 4)
go to Sidcup/speed 0/reverse
speed 2 (go to Euston)/etc etc

The students have written a computer program that also sits in the computer memory. This program is started by the operator at the computer console and from then on it looks after all eight trains, keeping a note of where they have got to on their own particular list of commands.

Here's how it works

All along the track are scattered about 45 little magnetic sensors. When your engine goes over one of these sensors the magnet glued to the underneath of the locomotive causes an electric pulse to go to the computer.

The computer then checks to see which engine is likely to have been at that point on the layout and then obeys the next command for that engine.

One of two separate things can happen. Your train may require to go into the next section of track. To do this the points must be set correctly and this will be done. But if another train is already occupying the next section you will have to wait, so the power is turned off and your engine skids to a halt.

When the next section is clear then your locomotive can go forward, and in its turn, the section behind you will be released so that other trains can use it.

What else can it do?

There are endless variations on this theme. For example in one of the programs there are no set routes for trains and the program will take any route that happens to be free. In yet another program the speed control is very accurate so that engines gently accelerate and gently slow down, more like in real life. It all depends on the cunning of the programmer. Many of the projects will require some rewiring or the use of extra electronics. All this is done by the computer.

The student could be you! If you would like to learn about electronic control at Newcastle why not ask one of the people on the stand for details, or contact

Dr. John Lloyd Computing Laboratory, University of Newcastle-upon-Tyne, Claremont Tower, Claremont Road, Newcastle-upon-Tyne.

Sponsored by CAP-CPP,
the world's largest software house
for microelectronics.

5 United States
AD Container Corporation of America
DIR/DES Jeff Barnes
COPY Rosalie Shonfeld
calendar/invitation to united fresh fruit &
vegetable show, calendrier/invitation pour
une exposition de fruits et légumes
Kalendar/Einladung zu Frucht und
Gemüseausstellung

6 Italy
AG La Rinascente Ufficio Pubblicità
DIR/DES Ettore Mariani
ILL Claudio Doveri
department store, magasin, Warenhaus

7 Brazil
AD Sao Paulo Alpargatas
AG Standard, Ogilvy & Mather
DIR Pierre Affonso Rousselet
ILL Marchi
COPY Laerth Pedrose
tennis shoes

8a-c Great Britain
AD Reebok International Ltd
AG Choice Advertising
DIR/DES Barry Oakes
ILL Tom Bowers
COPY Barry Oakes
athletics shoes

4

5

6

7

8c

8a

8b

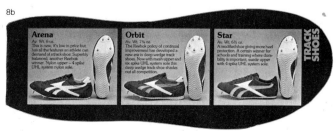

**Direct Mail
Brochures
Broschüren**

1a-e Germany
AD/COPY Presse und Werbeamt Wuppertal
DES Jris vom Hof
tourism

2 Canada
AD National Ballet of Canada
AG Raymond Lee and Associates Ltd
DIR/DES Raymond Lee
PHOTO Garth Scheuer (cover)
ballet

3a-b Italy
AD Schiffini SpA Ceparana
AG Studio Elle
DIR Ennio Lucini
ILL Alessandro Antonini, Aurelio Barbareschi,
Renzo Bazzani
COPY Ennio Lucini
catalogue

4 Great Britain
AD Race Furniture Ltd
AG Unit Five Design Ltd
DIR/DES Gus Hunnybun
PHOTO Dennis Hooker
COPY Lindsey Bareham
stacking chair system, système de chaises
qui s'emboitent, gestapelte stühle

5 Holland
AD De Phoenix
AG N.P.P.
DIR Eugène van Herpen
DES/ILL Tjeerd Wymem
COPY Peter van Tongeren
T-shirts and other textile-printings,
impressions pour T-shirts et autres textiles

1a

1b

1c

1d

1e

2

IDEEN AUS WUPPERTAL

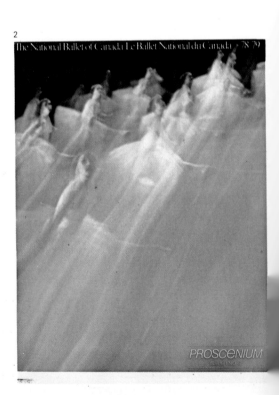

SCHIFFINI CUCINE DESIGN

3a

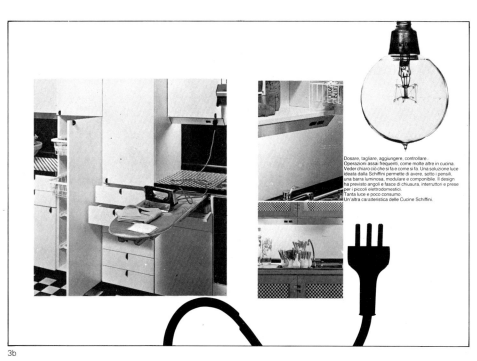

Dosare, tagliare, aggiungere, controllare.
Operazioni assai frequenti, come molte altre in cucina.
Veder chiaro ciò che si fa e come si fa. Una soluzione luce
ideata dalla Schiffini permette di avere, sotto i pensili,
una barra luminosa, modulare e componibile. Il design
ha previsto angoli e fasce di chiusura, interruttori e prese
per i piccoli elettrodomestici.
Tanta luce e poco consumo.
Un'altra caratteristica delle Cucine Schiffini.

3b

4

Tipster, a fully upholstered tubular linking, tip-up and stackable chair, is the first product from Race International Designs Limited. The company is an amalgamation of Sir Paul Reilly (Chairman), Ian Enslave (Managing Director) and Robert Heritage (Consultant Director).
Designed by Robert Heritage, the simplicity of the chair's design and its infinite range of accessories specially tailored to market uses, meets the demand for a highly versatile competitively priced mass use chair.
The Tipster's tip-up seat permits tighter rows of chairs thus giving more seating into a finite space. Its tip-up stacking potential is another major feature of the chair's mass use. With the seat flapped up and the chairs laid horizontally in specially designed trolleys, up to 25 chairs can be stacked with the seats down it nests tightly in low up to five. Its optional seat linking facility renders the chair suitable for single or mass use. Tipster is formed

from one continuous length of tube, available with a standard chromium plated finish or coloured nylon coating on request. The replaceable back and seat pads are available in Race's standard range of fire retardant, colour co-ordinated upholstery fabrics.
Suitable for home, audio-visuo, conference, reception, dining and other institutional uses, Tipster conforms to current fire regulations for public areas and British and International standards in terms of materials, dimensions and construction.

Tipster, stacked and with the seat tipped. Utilising the specially designed trolley, up to 25 chairs can be stacked combining stability with storage.

Tipster linked with writing tablets/bookshelves/ashtrays

race

TIPSTER

5

TREEDT
TOE TOT
DE ORDE
DER GROTE
VERSIERDERS

ORDE DER
GROTE
VERSIERDERS

Direct Mail
Brochures
Broschüren

1a-c Great Britain
AD John Laing Design Associates
AG John Nash & Friends
DIR John Nash
DES Charles Taylor
ILL Roy Coombes (cover) John Thirsk (inside)
for architectural designers, promotion pour
desinateurs architecture, Broschüre für
Architekten

1d Great Britain
AD Alcan Windows Ltd
AG John Nash & Friends
DIR/DES John Nash
ILL Fotopartners
COPY P. Ware
windows, fenêtres, fenste

1e-f Great Britain
AD MD Lighting
AG John Nash & Friends
DIR John Nash
DES/ILL Charles Taylor
light fittings, lumières, lampen

2 Sweden
AG Nordström-Grey
DIR Bruno Guilotte
ILL Ingvar Ericsson

3 Great Britain
AD Cork Manufacturing Co Ltd
AG Your Company by Design Ltd
DIR/DES Derrick Holmes
PHOTO James Mortimer
COPY Derrick Holmes/Elizabeth Neate
anti-vibration

4 Japan
AD Shokokusha Publishing Co Ltd
AG Takenobu Igarashi Design
DIR/DES/ILL Takenobu Igarashi
magazine cover, couverture de magazine,

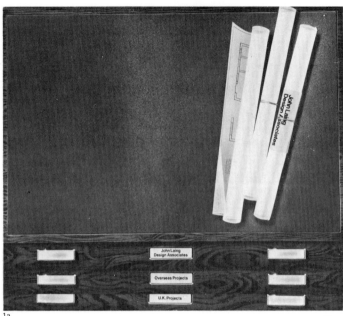

1a

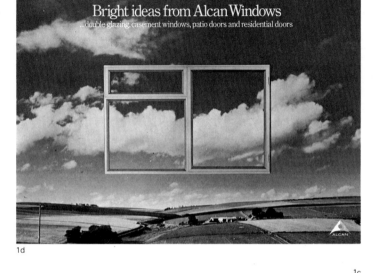

Bright ideas from Alcan Windows
... double glazing, casement windows, patio doors and residential doors

1d

1b

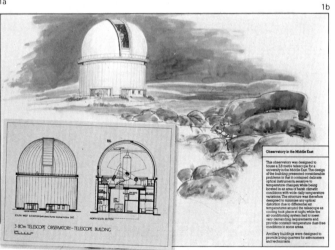

1c

1e

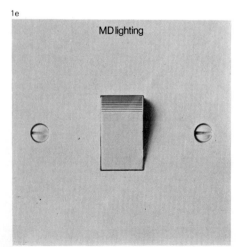

MD lighting

1f

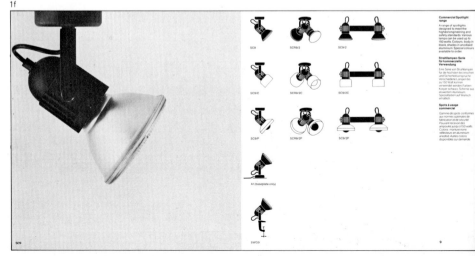

9

2a

THE SWEDISH APPROACH TO MINING.

2b 3

PROCESSING.

PROCESSING AT THE BEST LEVEL.
The world's deposits of known rich ore and clean mineral concentrations are fast disappearing. Mining companies are being forced to turn to lower grade deposits and extract minerals from these at lowest possible cost.
Sweden has been able to treat its low grade iron ore deposits and complex sulphide ores. This has been possible by the development of economic, sophisticated processes.
GIM knows that the experience of working with low grade deposits also qualifies us to beneficiate the rich ores at maximum recoveries.
An example of profitable process development is the extraction of a high grade apatite concentrate from high phosphorous iron ore. This technique was developed during World War II, when fertilizer supplies were cut off. Today the process is still working successfully in the Grängesberg iron ore plant producing very high grade apatite products used in the fertilizer industry.
GIM's processing know-how originated with systems used within the Gränges Group. Expertise has been added through recruitment from Swedish and foreign mining and processing companies. Our international projects have provided us with additional experience.

GIM can design and develop processes for new deposits or existing production. We work closely with the project's exploration, mining, engineering and marketing specialists to insure best technology and economic return.
GIM provides bench-scale and pilot plant testing in our own laboratories or in co-operation with research centers specializing in benefication, metallurgical or chemical processing.
New technology and processes are being developed in many countries—and GIM makes a special point of keeping up with worldwide developments. Promising innovations are tested in our own laboratories and plants, and results are made available to our clients.
GIM processing specialists can help keep your plant operating in the future.

Quality control is vital in all process industries. In mining, crude ore can vary significantly from one day to the next. Not only are there variations in chemical and mineralogical composition but also in physical properties.
In order to be processed most efficiently, crude ore must be prepared according to its quality and condition.
This preparation involves a complete grading and quality control system, which begins with geological mapping and continues through all phases of the production chain.
The methods employed include daily geological mapping, analysis of samples taken from blasting drill holes, automatic sampling in the transport system, and X-ray spectrometer analysis during processing. Results from the automatic X-ray analysis are fed back to the production system so that revisions can be made quickly to meet any changes in ore quality. Additional process control equipment is built into the crushing, blending, benefication and agglomeration plants.

HOW TO ADAPT THE ORE TO THE MARKET.

PRODUCT PLANNING.
You could have the world's richest ore body—but it is worth nothing if you cannot sell it.
That is where product planning comes in. Your products must meet the demands of the customers.
GIM will analyze your ore qualities and make thorough pre-feasibility studies based on current and future market forecasts. New ore products might be necessary—or there could be demands for modifications to the existing products.
A product development program is worked out based on the very complex factors of world mineral marketing.
Finally, there is trial production and delivery of samples for testing by selected customers and metallurgical laboratories.
This all forms the basis for a product program covering a specified period of time.
Sometimes you have to go even further. When it is not enough to adapt the ore to the market you have to refine the product and consequently plan for a higher degree of processing within the project.

WE KNOW HOW TO SELL IT.

SALES.
Selling is more than finding customers willing to pay the price. Today, producers must keep one step ahead of changing markets and the outside factors influencing demand.
Let us take an example: iron ore. In recent years, the market has been tough, as steel production world-wide slowed down.
At the same time, energy costs skyrocketed. For steel, the cost of coke doubled in a few years.
In an integrated steel mill, half of the total energy is consumed in the blast furnace. And up to 80 percent of the pig iron cost is for raw material.
Obviously, producers must tailor-make ore qualities to meet new energy demands.
GIM has been selling different ores for many years and also has in-house knowledge of marketing of developed metals.

GIM keeps its clients fully informed of market conditions. We follow technical developments of present and potential customers so that we can offer the right product at the right time at the right price.
Usually, the major part of production is sold through long-term contracts, covering specified quantities.
However, before entering such contracts, the seller must carefully consider advantages of retaining certain quantities for the free market.
GIM can handle the entire selling procedure. This involves drafting of contracts and documents, arranging for shipping on long and short term basis, supervising shipping, managing sampling and weighing, arranging analyses exchange with buyers, and handling invoicing.

4

建築の技術　ARCHITECTURAL PRODUCT-ENGINEERING

施工 12　1978 No.152

評論「街をつくる，家をつくる技術」大野勝彦
施工記録：新都心6番目の超高層―新宿野村ビルの施工―①「建築の概要と土工事」
技術レポート：ダブルスパイラル組立鉄筋による設計と施工――①
技術レポート：仕上工事における搬送作業の効率化
特別記事：「建築費指数集録」に見る変動と推移―建設
工業経営研究会30年間の成果
建築技術史を見る：甦る明治建築―熊本高等工業講堂を住宅に―西　和夫
連載：施工計画資料集成㉟―仮設設備および仮
設機構「揚重・運搬設備―水平運搬機器」
ディテール・シート：建築の納まりと施工―壁㊿「合成樹脂エマルション系複層模様吹付け材（吹付けタイルE）仕上」
時事解説：建設労働をめぐる安全衛生上の間問題と対策の方向―北山宏幸
続・伝統の工具㉑「1寸4分だたきのみ」千代鶴是秀作
海外文献ダイジェスト：スリップフォーム工法
気象：外装吹付け材の寒中施工による故障
How to VE：「エレベーターシャフト内足足座の改善」「スラブ型枠組立・解体工法の改善」
特許情報：「建造物架構法」

Control Vibration with Cork
The cheapest, simplest and most efficient method

Vibration can make working conditions on the shop floor very unpleasant
"My head is buzzing— vibration makes my working day a nightmare"

Vibration can be transmitted to other parts of the plant and into the offices
"Even up in my office, I can feel those machines vibrating, and they give me a headache"

Machinery vibration can be transmitted to the fabric of a building and cause structural damage, both expensive and unnecessary

Isolate your machinery and control vibration with Cork—the cheapest, simplest and most efficient method

Direct Mail
Brochures
Broschüren

1a-b Brazil
AD Varig Brazilian Airlines
DIR Clive Gay
travel brochure, livriet de voyage, Reise
prospekt

2 Denmark
AD DSB
AG Arbmann 5
DIR Bent Jacobsen
ILL Jesper Wanting
the DSB train today, le train DSB
d'aujourd'hui, Eisenbahnreklame

3a-b India
AD Air-India
AG Air-India Art Studiö
DES S.S. Dabholkar
DES/ILL C.V. Kamer
tourism

4a-b Great Britain
AD Matrex Ltd
AG Peter Proto Associates
DIR Peter Proto
DES Peter Proto and John Bodsworth
P.HOTO Fred Mancini
promotional brochure and stationery for new
system building, jeuiller de promotion et
paperene pour un nouveau système de
construction, prospekt für neues Bausystem

4c Great Britain
AD Adam Rouilly
AG Peter Proto Associates
DIR Peter Proto
DES Peter Proto and Jon Bodsworth
catalogue, catalogue

5 Japan
AD Matsushita Electric Ind.
AG CDP Japan Ltd
DIR Takaaki Ohtani
DES Shizuo Takahashi
PHOTO Masami Hagiwara
COPY David Gribbin
technical catalogue

1a

1b

2

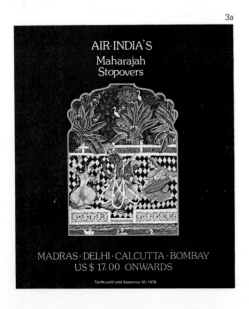

3a

3b

māt'rex *n.* versatile, multi purpose building method, mass produced (economical), lightweight (easy to erect), permanent (high quality) **steel frame**

4a

components

The Matrex Twin-Beam frame has been designed to provide maximum standardisation of components and fixings and this principle has been adhered to rigidly throughout its development.

Only two bolt sizes are used and a wide range of performance has been achieved with only two standard beam depths and three different column cross sections.
All components are part numbered and are therefore easy to identify and assemble.

A special feature of the Matrex Twin-Beam frame is that components forming roofs and floors may be pre-assembled at ground level on the building site or delivered to site in fully assembled condition for rapid erection.

lightweight

One of the essential design criteria for the Matrex Twin-Beam frame was that components should be lightweight and therefore easy to handle. In addition it was appreciated that lightness would produce other secondary benefits.
By using cold-rolled steel channel sections combined in the unique Matrex Twin-Beam manner the original criterion has been met together with a reduction in the weight of the structure and ultimate foundation loads.
A saving in foundation costs is of obvious benefit. A reduction in the construction programme is achieved and with a suspended floor, service distribution under the building can be simplified to show further economies.
Use of lightweight components eliminates or reduces the need for mechanical handling equipment and simplifies freighting, a particularly important feature for overseas projects.

4b

4c

5

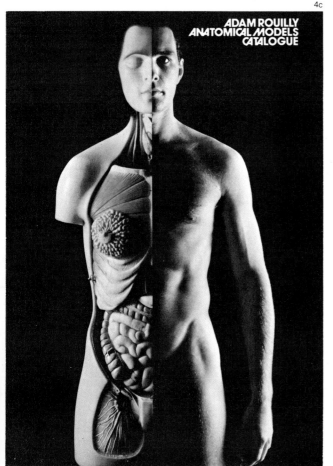

ADAM ROUILLY
ANATOMICAL MODELS
CATALOGUE

Technics
High Fidelity Bausteine

**Direct Mail
Brochures
Broschüren**

1a-b Great Britain
AD Eley-Witton, Birmingham
AG Kynoch Graphic Design
DIR/DES Len Harvey
PHOTO Brian Grainger
150 years anniversary, 150 ans
d'anniversaire, 150. jahrestag

2a-b Great Britain
AD Gavin Martin Ltd
AG Trickett & Webb Ltd
DIR Lynn Trickett/Brian Webb
DES Lyn Trickett/Brian Webb/Andrew
Thomas
10th anniversary mailing, 10. jahrestag

3a-c Great Britain
AD Volvo Concessionaires Ltd
AG Trickett & Webb Ltd
DIR Lyn Trickett/Brian Webb
DES Lynn Trickett/Brian Webb/Colin Sands
ILL John Ireland
launch mailing for car model, pour lancer un
modèle de voiture, neues Automodell

4a-c Great Britain
AD (a) Huckle Tweddell Architects
(b, c) Ironbridge trust
AG Minale, Tattersfield & Partners
DES M. Minale/Brian Tattersfield/Alex
Maranzano
promotional booklet, jeuillet de promotion

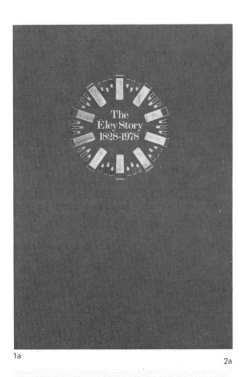

1a

1b

2b

3a

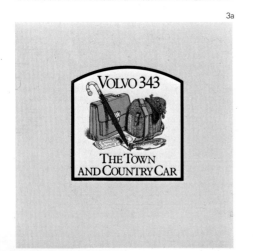

3b

3c

2a

Huckle Tweddell Partnership

The Partnership, which is a long established one, has a broad based experience of all types of architectural work, and at the present time consists of a staff of 50.

In the United Kingdom the Partnership has earned a high reputation for work in the field of Commercial and Industrial Building, and some of the foremost national companies are numbered amongst its clients. Great importance is attached to a close relationship with clients to ensure that requirements are fully met.

Particular emphasis is given to cost planning and control during the design process, and to proper programming and contract management during the building period. To assist in the Partnership is used to working in close and harmonious relationship with other specialist consultants forming the design team.

Within the Partnership's London based, it has long undertaken work overseas, especially in the Middle East, Central Africa and the West Indies. An office with a Resident Partner was established in 1975 in the Sultanate of Oman.

In addition to this, much of the recent work on the Middle East and elsewhere has been carried out under the name of Associated Design Consultants, a Consortium specially formed by the Partnership for the purpose. The Consortium consists of Civil and Structural Engineers, Heating, Ventilating, Air Conditioning and Plant Engineers, Architects and Quantity Surveyors, having a combined professional staff in excess of 200. The work of the constituent members of the Consortium covers a wide field of general civil engineering and building work, of which they have had extensive experience of all major types, both at home and overseas.

John Keith Hubert
Dipl Arch FRIBA ARAIA
Senior Partner

Jack Desmond Chamberlain
Dipl Arch ARIBA
Partner

Kenneth Ernest Fenson
AA Dipl ARIBA
Partner

Miles Park
MA AA Dipl ARIBA
Partner

Cyril John Bramley
Dipl Arch ARIBA ARAeS
Partner

Music School for the Haberdashers' Aske's School, Elstree

Primary School at Doha, Kuwait for the Ministry of Education, Kuwait

Assembly Building at Raynes Park for Cubitt Estates & Property Development Company Limited and Tenanted by Decca Navigator Company Limited

4a

4b

Living in the Ironbridge Gorge

4c

No account of the area is complete without reference to the work of the Ironbridge Gorge Museum Trust in protecting and restoring the local relics of the Industrial Revolution. Its famous museums within the area are now attracting international acclaim and those who have been to the Blists Hill Open Air Museum, or the award-winning Coalport China Museum, have seen how history can be brought alive.

**Direct Mail
Brochures
Broschüren**

1 Great Britain
AD ICI Plastics
AG Stuart & Knight Ltd
DIR/DES Jeremy Knight
ILL ICI Photographics Dept.
thermoplastic materials,

2 Great Britain
AD Honeywell
AG Gavin Healey Design
DIR/DES Gavin Healey
process automation training centre Europe,
centre d'apprentissage pour le
développement de l'automation

3 Great Britain
AD ICL Dataskil
AG David Harris Consultant Design
DIR/DES David Harris
ILL FNG Clarke Ltd
folder computer software company literature,
dépliant pour documentation de companie de
computer software

4 Great Britain
AD Milton Keynes Development Corporation
DES Jon Willcocks/A Ping-Ki Chan
PHOTO Peter Higgins
industrial literature
documentation industrielle

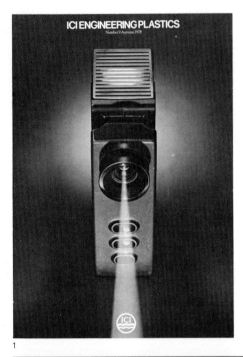

1

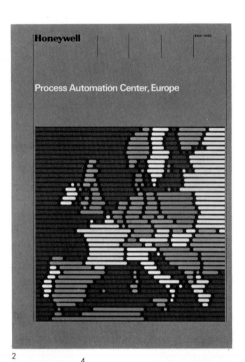

2

4

3

5

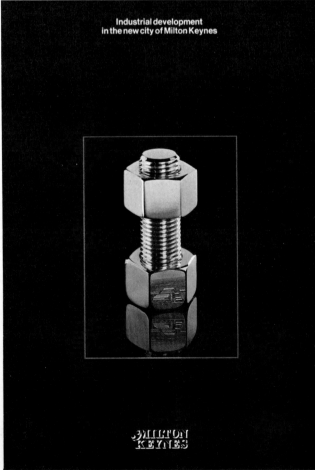

5 Germany
AD Fasson, Avery International Company
AG SSM Werbeagentur
DIR Willibald Fuchs
DES Erasmus Schlammer
ILL Klaus Spielkamp
self adhesive materials, selbstklebende
Materialen

6a-b Great Britain
AD Tarmac Group Wolverhampton
AG Michael Davighi Associates
DIR Paul Nichols
DES John Davies/Paul Nichols
ILL John Davies
history of tarmac group, historie d'une
companie de tarmac, Gestuchte einer
Teerfirma

7 United States
AD Massachusetts Institute of Technology
AG MIT Design Services
DES Nancy C. Pokross
PHOTO Ralph Mercer

8 Denmark
AD Spacebuild Systems AS
ag Benton & Bowles
DIR/DES John Andersen
ILL Von Cappelen
construction system, système de
construction

168-169

6a

6b

7

8

**Direct Mail
Brochures
Broschüren**

1a-d Japan
AD Zen Environmental Design
AG Takenobu Igarashi Design
DIR Takenobu Igarashi
DES Takenobu Igarashi/Yoshitsuyo Noma
company brochure, brochure d'une companie

2 Germany
AD Viessmann Werke
AG/DES Stankowski & Partners
factory prospectus

3 Canada
AD Ontario Hydro
AG Gingko Design Ltd
DIR/DES Harry Ägensky
series of three booklets on energy
conservation, série de trois livrets sur la
conservation de l'énergie

4 Germany
AD Hostmann Steinberg
AG Atelier Noth & Hauer
DIR/DES Volker Noth, Cordes Hauer, Peter
Sodemann
ILL Hartwig Klappert
printing inks, encres pour impression,
Druckfarben

1a

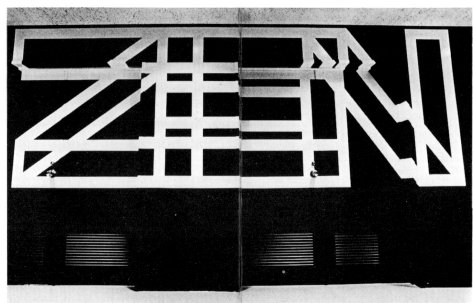

1b

2

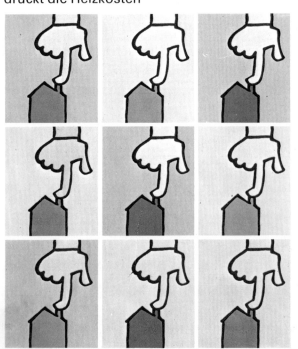

3

1c

1d

4

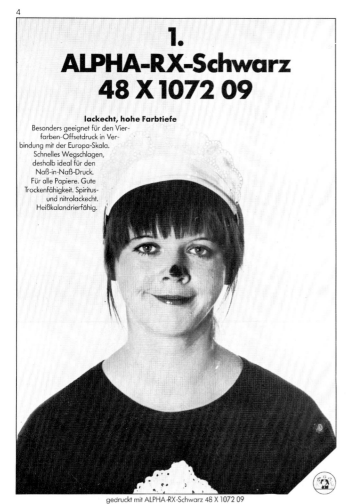

1.
ALPHA-RX-Schwarz
48 X 1072 09

lackecht, hohe Farbtiefe

Besonders geeignet für den Vier-
farben-Offsetdruck in Ver-
bindung mit der Europa-Skala.
Schnelles Wegschlagen,
deshalb ideal für den
Naß-in-Naß-Druck.
Für alle Papiere. Gute
Trockenfähigkeit. Spiritus-
und nitrolackecht.
Heißkalandrierfähig.

gedruckt mit ALPHA-RX-Schwarz 48 X 1072 09

2.
ALPHA-temp-Schwarz
49 Q 7777 09

schnell wegschlagend

In den meisten Fällen völlig
bestäubungsfrei auf Ein- und
Mehrfarbenmaschinen zu
verdrucken. Sehr gute Farbtiefe und ansprechender
Glanz. Durch das schnelle
Wegschlagen und
Trocknen ist eine
rasche Weiterver-
arbeitung der Drucke
möglich. Nicht lack-
echt. Für alle Papiere
geeignet.

gedruckt mit ALPHA-temp-Schwarz 49 Q 7777 09

1a-b United States
AD Moffatt & Nichol
AG The Weller Institute for the Cure of Design
DIR Don Weller
DES Don Weller, Chikako Matsubayashi
ILL Chikako Matsubayashi, Doug Reeder
COPY Bruce Russel
port and harbour engineers, ingénieurs pour ports maritimes

2 Great Britain
AD Welsh Office
AG Central Office of Information
DIR P. Daniell
DES Michael Reid
ILL Michael Whitland
technical manual for architects, planners etc.
manuel technique pour architectes, unbarriste, etc., technisches Handbuch für Architekten

3a Great Britain
AD Ordnance Survey
AG HMSO Graphic Design
DIR Philip Marriage
ILL Gary Hincks, David Williams
monastic Britain, Grande Bretagne monacale, die Klöster Englands

3b Great Britain
AD HMSO
AG HMSO/Edinburgh
DES/ILL James Cairns
oil report

Expansion of world trade:
the key to sharing of Earth's bounty.
Modernization of ports:
the key to expanded trade.
Planning port modernization:
our contribution to world betterment.

1a

THE HARBOR

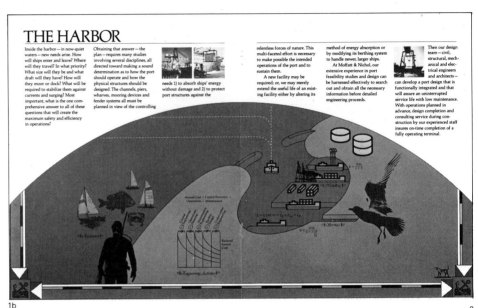

Inside the harbor – in now-quiet waters – new needs arise. How will ships enter and leave? Where will they travel? In what priority? What size will they be and what draft will they have? How will they moor or dock? What will be required to stabilize them against currents and surging? Most important, what is the one comprehensive answer to all of these questions that will create the maximum safety and efficiency in operations?

Obtaining that answer – the plan – requires many studies involving several disciplines, all directed toward making a sound determination as to how the port should operate and how the physical structures should be designed. The channels, piers, wharves, mooring devices and fender systems all must be planned in view of the controlling needs 1) to absorb ships' energy without damage and 2) to protect port structures against the

relentless forces of nature. This multi-faceted effort is necessary to make possible the intended operations of the port and to sustain them.

A new facility may be required; or, we may merely extend the useful life of an existing facility either by altering its method of energy absorption or by modifying its berthing system to handle newer, larger ships.

At Moffatt & Nichol, our extensive experience in port feasibility studies and design can be harnessed effectively to search out and obtain all the necessary information before detailed engineering proceeds.

Then our design team – civil, structural, mechanical and electrical engineers and architects – can develop a port design that is functionally integrated and that will assure an uninterrupted service life with low maintenance. With operations planned in advance, design completion and consulting service during construction by our experienced staff insures on-time completion of a fully operating terminal.

1b

2

Car parking

Parking spaces
Where provision for parking is made, spaces should be reserved for disabled drivers and passengers. The preferred width for a parking bay is 3 000mm and the area should be substantially level.
Avoid siting parking spaces on the off-side of a one way street. The wheelchair user normally gets out on the near-side and would not wish to alight in a traffic lane.

Position
Spaces which are reserved for the use of disabled people should be those which are nearest to an entrance to a building, shopping precinct or other facility.

Signposting
All entrances to car parks with reserved spaces for disabled drivers and passengers should be clearly signposted to this effect. Additionally, there should be clear direction signs for reaching the reserved areas, and the ground set aside for this purpose should be adequately marked out.

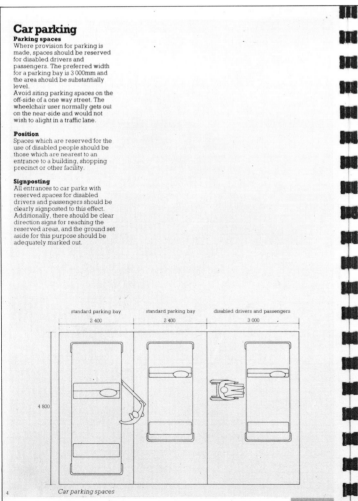

Car parking spaces

4

5

4 Great Britain
AD Edinburgh University Student
Publications Board
AG Wide Art Studies
DIR/DES James Hutcheson
'New Edinburgh Review'

5 Denmark
AD Modulex Sign Systems
AG Niels Hartmann
DES Niels Hartmann
product brochure, brochure sur un produit

6 Great Britain
AD BBC Enterprises
AG Design Dept. BBC Enterprises
DIR/DES Robin Ward
COPY Ada Wood
BBC TV Shakespeare Series,

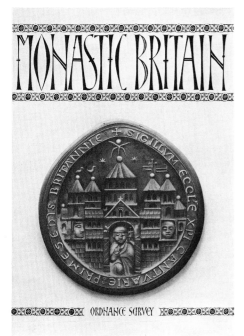

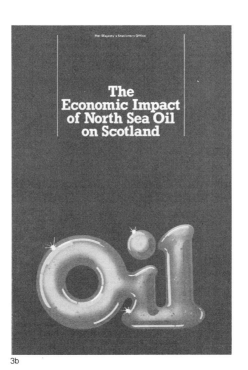

3a

3b

4

5

6

1a-g United States
AD Smith Kline & French Labs.
AG Smith Kline & French Labs.
DIR Alan J. Klawans
DES (a-b) Bruno Mease (c) Jim Lekis
      (d-g) Jonson Pedersen Hinrichs
ILL (a-b) Bob Giodomenica (c) Joel Freid
COPY Leonard Aulenbach
tranquilizer, tranquilisant, Beruhigungsmittel

2 Australia
AD ER Squibb & Sons
AG Flett Henderson & Arnold Graphic Design
DIR/DES Richard Henderson
pharmaceutical products

3 Canada
AD Hoffman-La Roche Ltd
AG Rolf Harder & Associates
DIR Rolf Harder, Karl Hardy
DES Rolf Harder
mailing piece for doctors,

4 United States
AD Smith, Kline & French Labs.
DIR J. Robert Parker
DES Talone & Labrasca
ILL Steve Tarantel/Seymour Mednick
COPY Gerri Henwood
for treatment of infection, traitement
pour l'infection

5 Spain
AD Laboratorios Jorba
AG/DIR/DES Enric Huguet
pharmaceutical products (antibiotics),
produits pharmaceutiques (anti biotiques)

1a

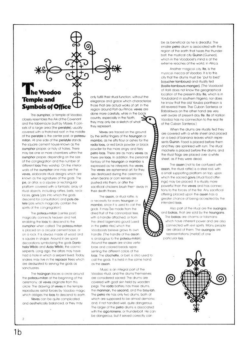

1b

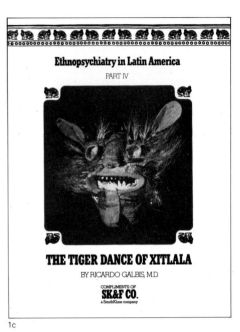

1c

1d

1e

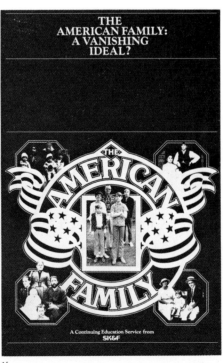

1f

1g

6a-b Great Britain
AD Nedo
AG Lock/Pettersen Ltd
DIR David Lock
DES David Lock/Steve Franks
ILL Mick Brownfield
COPY John Simmons
the government's industrial strategy,
stratégie industrielle du gouvernement, die
industrielle strategie der Regierung

7a-c Brazil
AD Secretaria da Fazenda do Estado de
Pernambuco
AG Cunha Lima e Associados
DIR/DES/ILL Guilherme Cunha Lima
report of the Treasury State Department,

2

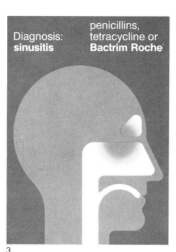

3

4

5

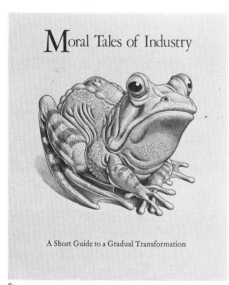

6a

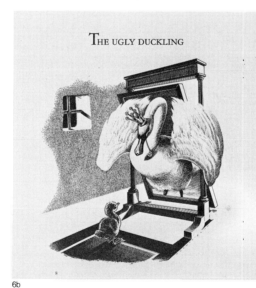

6b

7b

7c

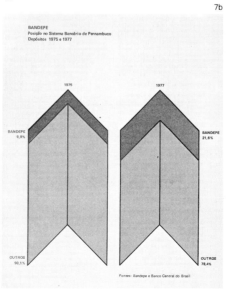

7a

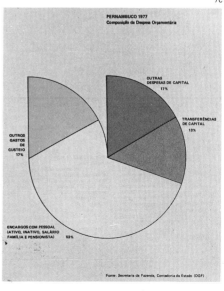

1 Canada
AD C & C Yachts Ltd
AG Rous & Mann Press Ltd
DIR/DES O.K. Schenk
ILL André Jubinville
annual report

2a-b Great Britain
AD Habitat Design Holdings Ltd
AG Conran Associates
DIR/DES Gavin Clive-Smith
ILL Ian Beck
COPY Ginny Pepper
annual review

3 Great Britain
AD European Molecular Biology Laboratories
AG Design Research Unit
DIR/DES Richard Dragun
annual report

4 Great Britain
AD Tootal Ltd
AG Hans Schleger and Associates
DIR Pat Schleger
DES Hans Schleger and Associates
ILL Alan Murgatroyd and others
prestige brochure, brochure de prestige

5a-b United States
AD Manufacturers Hanover Corporation
AG Harrison Associates
DIR Peter Harrison
DES Randee Rafkin-Rubin
ILL Barron Storey
COPY Manufacturers Hanover Corp.
annual report

6a-b Brazil
AD IBC Instituto Brasileiro do Café
AG P.A.Z. Criaçao e Communicaçao Ltda
DIR/DES Oswaldo Miranda
PHOTO Bruno Roberto
COPY Equipe IBC
annual report

1

2a

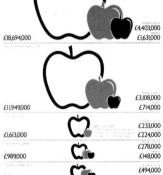

2b

3

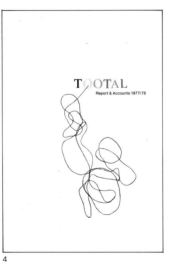

4

5a

5b

6a

6b

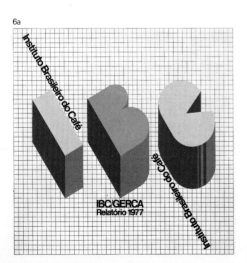

7 Great Britain
AD Cap-CPP Ltd
AG Butler Cornfield Dedman Ltd
DIR/DES Paul Butler
ILL David Bull (cover)
annual report

8 United States
AD Tally Industries Inc
AG Runyan & Rice
DIR Robert Runyan
DES Jim Berte
ILL Marvin Silver
annual report

9 United States
AD St Joe Minerals Corporation
AG Corporate Annual Reports, Inc
DIR/DES Len Fury
ILL Gary Gladstone
COPY Bob Peckim

10 United States
AD Standard Brands Paint Company
AG The Weller Institute for the Cure of
Design
DIR Don Weller
DES Don Weller, Chikako Matsubayashi
ILL Ron Scott
COPY Sheldon Weinstein
annual report

11 United States
AD National Semiconductor Corporation
AG Ken Parkhurst & Associates Inc
DIR/DES Ken Parkhurst
hotel and marina in Florida

7

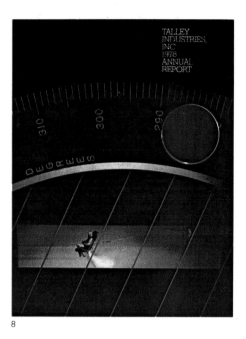

8

9

10

11

Direct Mail
Brochures
Broschüren

1a-c Italy
AD Assessorato alla Cultura del Comune di Roma
AG Giuliano Vittori
DES Giuliano Vittori
daily programme for film festival, programme journalier d'un festival du film, Tagesprogramm für Film festival

2 Germany
AD ARW Arbeitsgemeinschaft Rundfunkwerbung
STUDIO Jon Pahlow
DIR/DES/ILL Jon Pahlow
TV play, pièce pour le télévision

3a-b Hong Kong
AD Urban Council Hong Kong
AG S S Design & Production
DIR Kan Tai-Keung/Cheung Shu-Sun
DES Cheung Shu-Sun/Kan Tai-Keung
souvenir programme of Festival of Asian Arts, programme souvenir du Festival des Artes Asiatiques

4a-b United States
AD Central Penna Arts Festival
AG Lanny Sommese Design
DIR/DES/ILL Lanny Sommese
Arts Festival

5 Singapore
AD Yippee! Magazine
AG Art Direction Creative Workshop
children's magazine, magazine pour enfants, Kinderzeitschrift

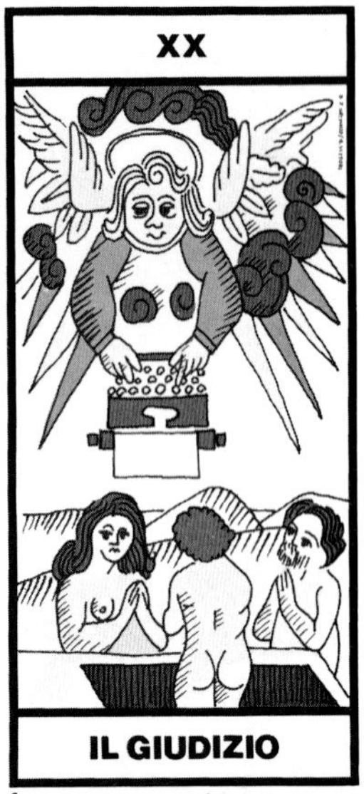

1a

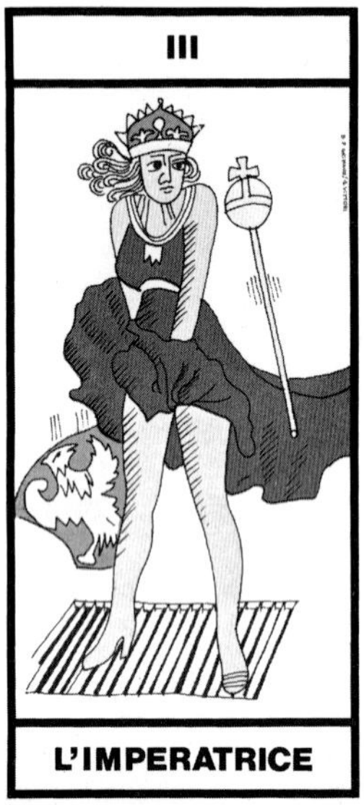

1b

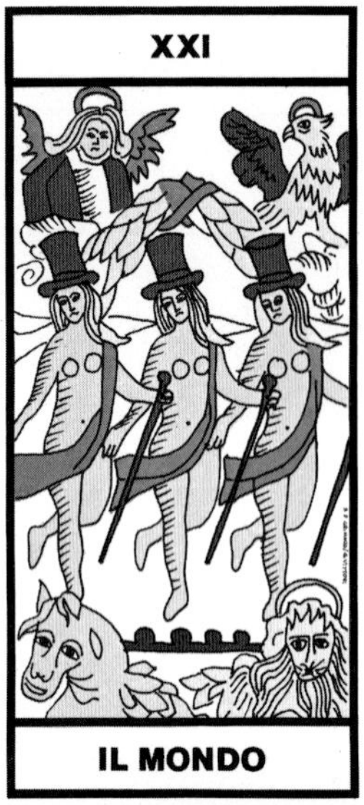

1c

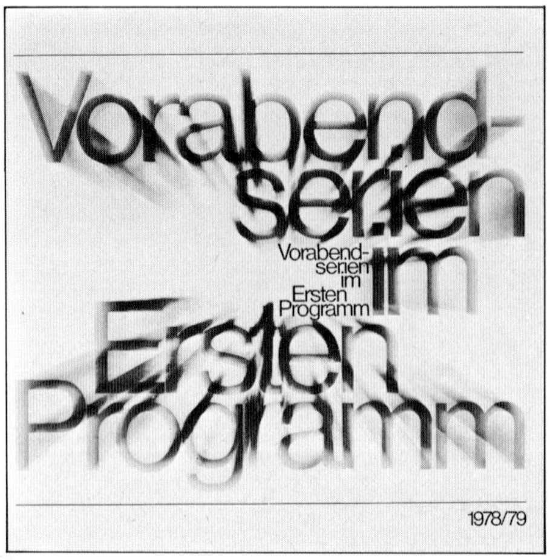

2

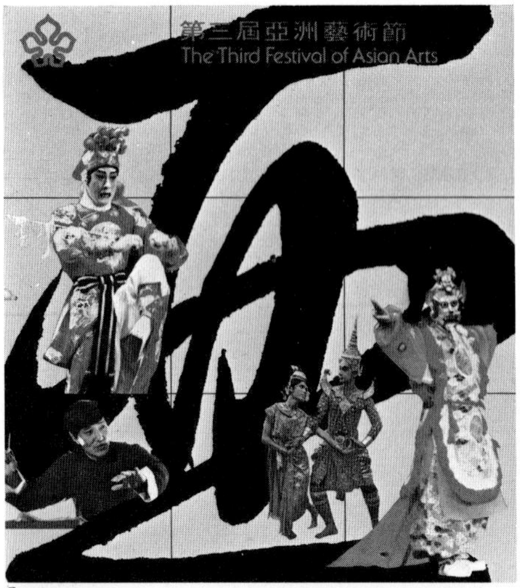

3a

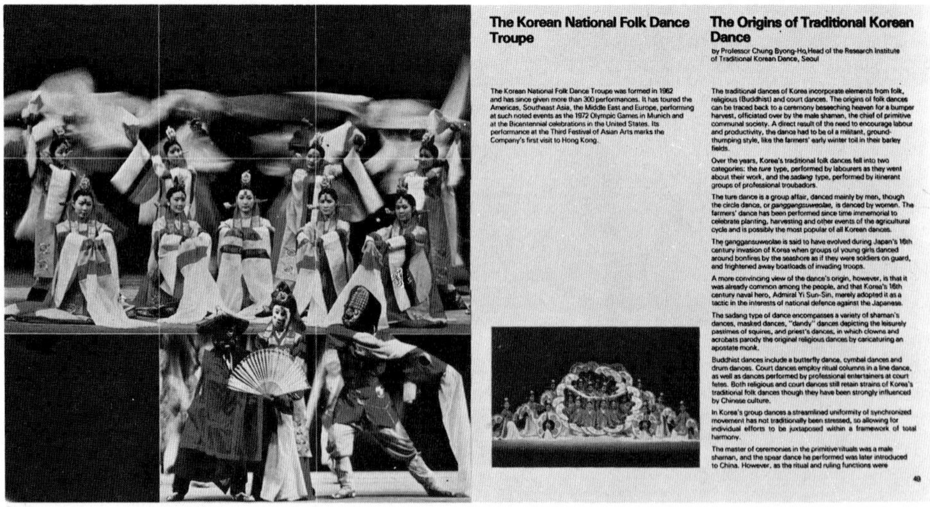

The Korean National Folk Dance Troupe

The Korean National Folk Dance Troupe was formed in 1962 and has since given more than 300 performances. It has toured the Americas, Southeast Asia, the Middle East and Europe, performing at such noted events as the 1972 Olympic Games in Munich and at the Bicentennial celebrations in the United States. Its performance at the Third Festival of Asian Arts marks the Company's first visit to Hong Kong.

The Origins of Traditional Korean Dance

by Professor Chung Byong-Ho, Head of the Research Institute of Traditional Korean Dance, Seoul

The traditional dances of Korea incorporate elements from folk, religious (Buddhist) and court dances. The origins of folk dances can be traced back to a ceremony beseeching heaven for a bumper harvest, officiated over by the male shaman, the chief of primitive communal society. A direct result of the need to encourage labour and productivity, the dance had to be of a militant, ground-thumping style, like the farmers' early winter toil in their barley fields.

Over the years, Korea's traditional folk dances fell into two categories: the *ture* type, performed by labourers as they went about their work, and the *sadang* type, performed by itinerant groups of professional troubadors.

The ture dance is a group affair, danced mainly by men, though the circle dance, or *ganggangsuweolae*, is danced by women. The farmers' dance has been performed since time immemorial to celebrate planting, harvesting and other events of the agricultural cycle and is possibly the most popular of all Korean dances.

The gangganṣuweolae is said to have evolved during Japan's 16th century invasion of Korea when groups of young girls danced around bonfires by the seashore as if they were soldiers on guard, and frightened away boatloads of invading troops.

A more convincing view of the dance's origin, however, is that it was already common among the people, and that Korea's 16th century naval hero, Admiral Yi Sun-Sin, merely adopted it as a tactic in the interests of national defence against the Japanese.

The sadang type of dance encompasses a variety of shaman's dances, masked dances, "dandy" dances depicting the leisurely pastimes of squires, and priest's dances, in which clowns and acrobats parody the original religious dances by caricaturing an apostate monk.

Buddhist dances include a butterfly dance, cymbal dances and drum dances. Court dances employ ritual columns in a line dance, as well as dances performed by professional entertainers at court fetes. Both religious and court dances still retain strains of Korea's traditional folk dances though they have been strongly influenced by Chinese culture.

In Korea's group dances a streamlined uniformity of synchronized movement has not traditionally been stressed, so allowing for individual efforts to be juxtaposed within a framework of total harmony.

The master of ceremonies in the primitive rituals was a male shaman, and the spear dance he performed was later introduced to China. However, as the ritual and ruling functions were

49

3b

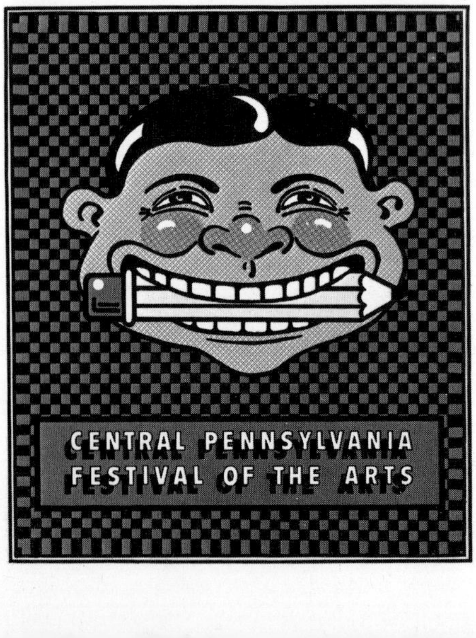

4a

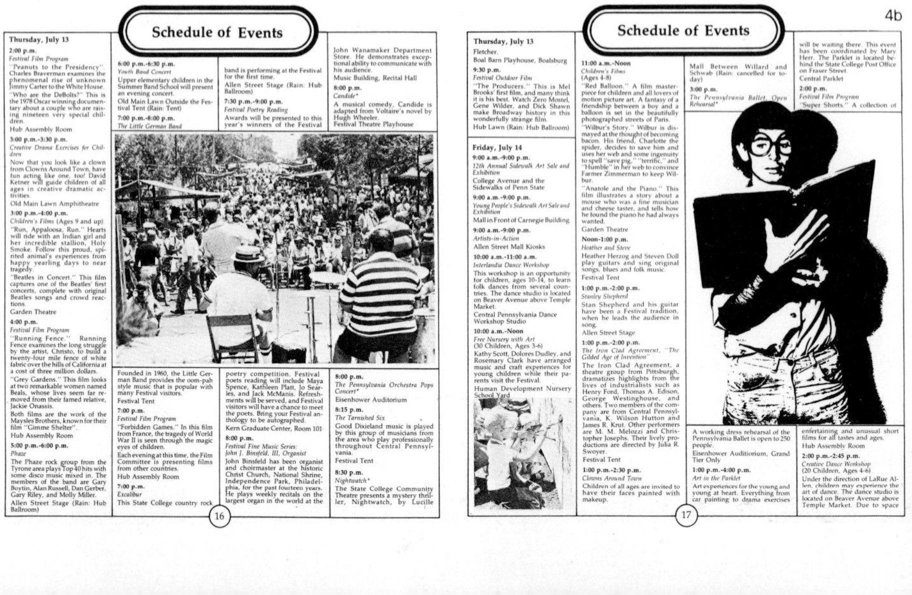

Schedule of Events

Thursday, July 13

2:00 p.m.
Festival Film Program
"Peanuts to the Presidency". Charles Braverman examines the phenomenal rise of unknown Jimmy Carter to the White House.
"Who are the DeBolts?" This is the 1978 Oscar winning documentary about a couple who are raising nineteen very special children.
Hub Assembly Room

3:00 p.m.-3:30 p.m.
Creative Drama Exercises for Children
Now that you look like a clown from Clowns Around Town, have fun acting like one, too! David Ketner will guide children of all ages in creative dramatic activities.
Old Main Lawn Amphitheatre

3:00 p.m.-4:00 p.m.
Children's Films (Ages 9 and up)
"Run, Appaloosa, Run." Hearts will ride with an Indian girl and her incredible stallion, Holy Smoke. Follow this proud, spirited animal's experiences from happy yearling days to near tragedy.
"Beatles in Concert." This film captures one of the Beatles' first concerts, complete with original Beatles songs and crowd reactions.
Garden Theatre

4:00 p.m.
Festival Film Program
"Running Fence." Running Fence examines the long struggle by the artist, Christo, to build a twenty-four mile fence of white fabric over the hills of California at a cost of three million dollars.
"Grey Gardens." This film looks at two remarkable women named Beals, whose lives seem far removed from their famed relative, Jackie Onassis.
Both films are the work of the Maysles Brothers, known for their film "Gimme Shelter".
Hub Assembly Room

5:00 p.m.-6:00 p.m.
Phaze
The Phaze rock group from the Tyrone area plays Top 40 hits with some disco music mixed in. The members of the band are Gary Boytin, Alan Russell, Dan Gerber, Gary Riley, and Molly Miller.
Allen Street Stage (Rain: Hub Ballroom)

6:00 p.m.-6:30 p.m.
Youth Band Concert
Upper elementary children in the Summer Band School will present an evening concert.
Old Main Lawn Outside the Festival Tent (Rain: Tent)

7:00 p.m.-8:00 p.m.
The Little German Band
Founded in 1960, the Little German Band provides the oom-pah style music that is popular with many Festival visitors.
Festival Tent

7:00 p.m.
Festival Film Program
"Forbidden Games." In this film from France, the tragedy of World War II is seen through the magic eyes of children.
Each evening at this time, the Film Committee is presenting films from other countries.
Hub Assembly Room

7:00 p.m.
Excalibur
This State College country rock band is performing at the Festival for the first time.
Allen Street Stage (Rain: Hub Ballroom)

7:30 p.m.-9:00 p.m.
Festival Poetry Reading
Awards will be presented to this year's winners of the Festival poetry competition. Festival poets reading will include Maya Spence, Kathleen Platt, Jo Searles, and Jack McManis. Refreshments will be served, and Festival visitors will have a chance to meet the poets. Bring your Festival anthology to be autographed.
Kern Graduate Center, Room 101

8:00 p.m.
Festival Fine Music Series: John J. Binsfeld, III, Organist
John Binsfeld has been organist and choirmaster at the historic Christ Church, National Shrine, Independence Park, Philadelphia, for the past fourteen years. He plays weekly recitals on the largest organ in the world at the John Wanamaker Department Store. He demonstrates exceptional ability to communicate with his audience.
Music Building, Recital Hall

8:00 p.m.
*Candide**
A musical comedy, Candide is adapted from Voltaire's novel by Hugh Wheeler.
Festival Theatre Playhouse

8:00 p.m.
*The Pennsylvania Orchestra Pops Concert**
Eisenhower Auditorium

8:15 p.m.
The Tarnished Six
Good Dixieland music is played by this group of musicians from the area who play professionally throughout Central Pennsylvania.
Festival Tent

8:30 p.m.
*Nightwatch**
The State College Community Theatre presents a mystery thriller, Nightwatch, by Lucille

16

Thursday, July 13
Fletcher.
Boal Barn Playhouse, Boalsburg

9:30 p.m.
Festival Outdoor Film
"The Producers." This is Mel Brooks' first film, and many think it is his best. Watch Zero Mostel, Gene Wilder, and Dick Shawn make Broadway history in this wonderfully strange film.
Hub Lawn (Rain: Hub Ballroom)

Friday, July 14

9:00 a.m.-9:00 p.m.
12th Annual Sidewalk Art Sale and Exhibition
College Avenue and the Sidewalks of Penn State

9:00 a.m.-9:00 p.m.
Young People's Sidewalk Art Sale and Exhibition
Mall in Front of Carnegie Building

9:00 a.m.-9:00 p.m.
Artists-in-Action
Allen Street Mall Kiosks

10:00 a.m.-11:00 a.m.
Interlandia Dance Workshop
This workshop is an opportunity for children, ages 10-14, to learn folk dances from several countries. The dance studio is located on Beaver Avenue above Temple Market.
Central Pennsylvania Dance Workshop Studio

10:00 a.m.-Noon
Free Nursery with Art
(30 Children, Ages 3-6)
Kathy Scott, Dolores Dudley, and Rosemary Clark have arranged music and craft experiences for young children while their parents visit the Festival.
Human Development Nursery School Yard

11:00 a.m.-Noon
Children's Films
(Ages 4-8)
"Red Balloon." A film masterpiece for children and all lovers of motion picture art. A fantasy of a friendship between a boy and a balloon is set in the beautifully photographed streets of Paris.
"Wilbur's Story." Wilbur is dismayed at the thought of becoming bacon. His friend, Charlotte the spider, decides to save him and uses her web and some ingenuity to spell "save pig," "terrific," and "Humble" in her web to convince Farmer Zimmerman to keep Wilbur.
"Anatole and the Piano." This film illustrates a story about a mouse who was a fine musician and cheese taster, and tells how he found the piano he had always wanted.
Garden Theatre

Noon-1:00 p.m.
Heather and Steve
Heather Herzog and Steven Doll play guitars and sing original songs, blues and folk music.
Festival Tent

1:00 p.m.-2:00 p.m.
Stanley Shepherd
Stan Shepherd and his guitar have been a Festival tradition, when he leads the audience in song.
Allen Street Stage

1:00 p.m.-2:00 p.m.
The Iron Clad Agreement, "The Gilded Age of Invention"
The Iron Clad Agreement, a theatre group from Pittsburgh, dramatizes highlights from the lives of industrialists such as Henry Ford, Thomas A. Edison, George Westinghouse, and others. Two members of the company are from Central Pennsylvania, K. Wilson Hutton and James R. Krut. Other performers are M. M. Melozzi and Christopher Josephs. Their lively productions are directed by Julia R. Swoyer.
Festival Tent

1:00 p.m.-2:30 p.m.
Clowns Around Town
Children of all ages are invited to have their faces painted with makeup.

Mall Between Willard and Schwab (Rain: cancelled for today)

3:00 p.m.
*The Pennsylvania Ballet, Open Rehearsal**
A working dress rehearsal of the Pennsylvania Ballet is open to 250 people.
Eisenhower Auditiorium, Grand Tier Only

1:00 p.m.-4:00 p.m.
Art in the Parklet
Art experiences for the young and young at heart. Everything from car painting to drama exercises will be waiting there. This event has been coordinated by Mary Herr. The Parklet is located behind the State College Post Office on Fraser Street.
Central Parklet

2:00 p.m.
Festival Film Program
"Super Shorts." A collection of entertaining and unusual short films for all tastes and ages.
Hub Assembly Room

2:00 p.m.-2:45 p.m.
Creative Dance Workshop
(20 Children, Ages 4-6)
Under the direction of LaRue Allen, children may experience the art of dance. The dance studio is located on Beaver Avenue above Temple Market. Due to space

17

4b

5

6

7

8

9

**Direct Mail
Brochures
Broschüren**

1a-c Germany
AD Druckfarbenfabrik Gebr. Schmidt
AG Olaf Leu Design & Partner
DIR/DES Olaf Leu, Fritz Hofrichter
printing inks

2a-b Germany
AD Druckfarbenfabrik Gebr-Schmidt
AG Olaf Leu Design & Partner
DIR Olaf Leu/Fritz Hofrichter
printing inks

3a-b Germany
AD Zanders Feinpapiere GmbH & Co
AG Schlüter Design/Zanders Werbeabteilung
paper manufacturers

3c Germany
AD Zanders Feinpapiere GmbH & Co
AG Werbeagentur Dorland/Zanders
Werbeabteilung
paper manufacturers

4a-b Germany
AD Main Klischee
AG/DES Dieter Fröbisch
colour separations, cliché

1a

1b

1c

Die Gewalt des Feuers
vernichtet Leben

Die feurrote Feuerwehr.
Signal des Alarms und der Gefahr

2a

2b

3a

CHROMOLUX
FRIENDSHIP COLLECTION

ZANDERS

3b

3c

5a-b Australia
AD Associated Pulp and Paper Mills Ltd
AG K.M. Campbell Advertising
DIR/DES R. Henderson
ILL R. Goode/R. Henderson
paper manufacturers

6a-b United States
AD Champion Papers
DIR Miho
DES/ILL Miho and others
paper manufacturers

4a-b

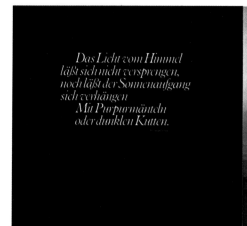

FIVE FACES OF GLOPAQUE

POSTERS

5a-b

Main Street Information

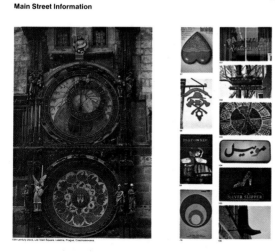

6a-b

Main Street: Smalltown, U.S.A.

Direct Mail
Brochures
Broschüren

1a-b Great Britain
AD Thames Television
AG Trickett & Webb Ltd
DIR Lynn Trickett & Brian Webb
DES Lynn Trickett/Brian Webb/Andrew Thomas
annual review, revue annuelle

1c-e Great Britain
AD Thames Television
AG Trickett & Webb Ltd
DIR Lynn Trickett and Brian Webb
DES Lynn Trickett/Brian Webb/Colin Sands
advance publicity material for TV programmes, publicité annonçant à l'avance des programmes de télévision, Aukündigung eines neuen programmes

1f Great Britain
AG Trickett & Webb Ltd
DIR Lynn Trickett/Brian Webb
DES Lynn Trickett/Brian Webb/Andrew Thomas
change of address, changement d'address, Adressenänderung

2a-b Spain
AD (a) Laboratorios Elmu SA
    (b) Laboratorios Dr. Estere
AG Pharma/Consult SA
DIR/DES Vincente Olmos
ILL Joan Enric
pharmaceuticals

3 United States
AD Theatre Project
AG Bill Kinser Design
DIR/DES/ILL Bill Kinser
newspaper, journal

1a

1b

2a   2b

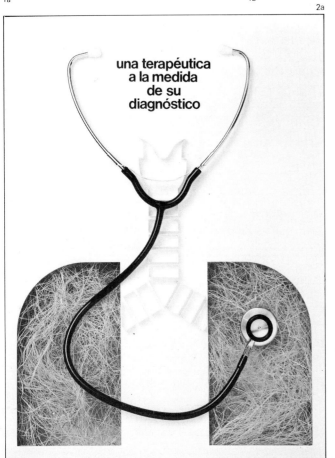

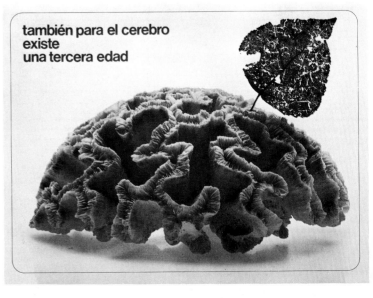

Thames Television

1

Number

IN
LIGHT
ENTERTAINMENT
SUPERIOR QUALITY

THIS PACK CONTAINS ONLY ACES

1c

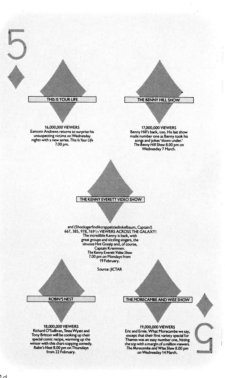

5

THIS IS YOUR LIFE

16,000,000 VIEWERS
Eamonn Andrews returns to surprise his unsuspecting victims on Wednesday nights with a new series. *This Is Your Life* 7.00 pm.

THE BENNY HILL SHOW

17,000,000 VIEWERS
Benny Hill's back, too. His last show made number one as Benny took his songs and jokes 'down under.' *The Benny Hill Show* 8.00 pm on Wednesday 7 March.

THE KENNY EVERETT VIDEO SHOW

and (Shocksgerfindlkcrapelziedinkelbaum, Captain!) 667, 385, 978, 769½ VIEWERS ACROSS THE GALAXY! The incredible Kenny is back, with great groups and sizzling singers, the sinuous Hot Gossip and, of course, Captain Kremmen. *The Kenny Everett Video Show* 7.00 pm on Mondays from 19 February.
Source: JICTAR

ROBIN'S NEST

18,000,000 VIEWERS
Richard O'Sullivan, Tessa Wyatt and Tony Britton will be cooking up their special comic recipe, warming up the winter with this chart-topping comedy. *Robin's Nest* 8.00 pm on Thursdays from 22 February.

THE MORECAMBE AND WISE SHOW

19,000,000 VIEWERS
Eric and Ernie. What Morecambe we say, except that their first variety special for Thames was an easy number one, hitting the top with a margin of a million viewers. *The Morecambe and Wise Show* 8.00 pm on Wednesday 14 March.

1d

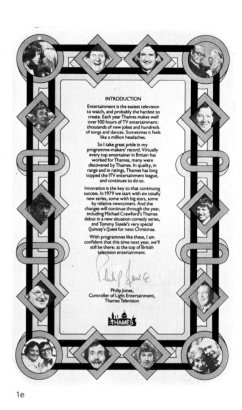

INTRODUCTION

Entertainment is the easiest television to watch, and probably the hardest to create. Each year Thames makes well over 100 hours of TV entertainment: thousands of new jokes and hundreds of songs and dances. Sometimes it feels like a million headaches.

So I take great pride in my programme-makers' record. Virtually every top entertainer in Britain has worked for Thames, many were discovered by Thames. In quality, in range and in ratings, Thames has long topped the ITV entertainment league, and continues to do so.

Innovation is the key to that continuing success. In 1979 we start with six totally new series, some with big stars, some by relative newcomers. And the changes will continue through the year, including Michael Crawford's Thames debut in a new situation comedy series, and Tommy Steele's very special *Quincey's Quest* for next Christmas.

With programmes like these, I am confident that this time next year, we'll still be there: at the top of British television entertainment.

Philip Jones,
Controller of Light Entertainment,
Thames Television

1e

1f

Theatre Project
BALTIMORE
N E W S P A P E R

Blackbird Christmas

In the midst of tinsel, fruitcake, and eggnog, somewhere between *The Nutcracker* and *The Messiah*, we hope that you will join us here at the Theatre Project for The Blackbird Theater's production of The Bread and Puppet's *Christmas Story*. Andy Trumpeter directs the play in the style of the medieval mystery dramas, using life-sized masked figures, hand puppets, and a larger-than-life angel.

Though the music and liturgy are contemporary, and the story is treated in a secular manner, the drama follows the account of the birth of Christ as told in *The Gospel According to Matthew*. It begins: "The book of the genealogy of Jesus Christ, the son of David, the son of Abraham and as it begins, each of the patriarchs takes a bow.

As in the medieval mystery plays, the characters and the symbolism are direct and clear. There are Joseph, Mary, and the Christ Child, the angels, the shepherds; the Wise Men are a mute figure — a three-headed mask worn by a single player; King Herod is unmistakably corrupt. Evil is unspeakably evil. The Good is all good, all powerful.

The Blackbird Theatre, our resident company, first performed its rendition of *The Christmas Story* in a church in Portland, Maine in 1970, and has continued to perform it every year since. According to Andy Trumpeter, the piece is now a Blackbird Christmas tradition. I think that it should become a Baltimore tradition als

DECEMBER						
19 Tues 8 p.m.	20 Wed 8 p.m.	21 Thurs 8 p.m.	22 Fri 8 p.m.	23 Sat. 4 p.m. 8 p.m.	24 Christmas Eve no perfs. today	25 Christmas day 4 p.m.

3

Greetings cards
Calendars
Cartes de voeux
Calendriers
Glückwunschkarten
Kalender

1 Brazil
AD Volkswagen do Brasil SA
AG Alcantara Machado Periscinoto
Communicaçoes Ltda
DIR Enido Angelo Michelini
PHOTO José Daloia Neto
COPY Ruy A. Duarte Gutierres
1979 Volkswagen calendar
Calendrier Volkswagen pour 1979

2 Mexico
AD Carton y papel de Mexico SA
DIR/DES Arje Geurts
calendar for papermills, calendrier pour
fabrique de papier, Papierfabrik

3a-b Germany
AD Institut für Angewante
Geowissenschaften
DIR/DES Eckhard Neumann
ILL Dr Georg Gerster, NASA
COPY Dr Klaus Völger, editor
geological institute

4 Germany
AD Hostman Steinberg
DIR Noth & Hauer
PHOTO Hartwig Klappert
printing inks

1

2

3a

3d

5 Poland
AD P.P. Totalizator Sportowy
DES Edward Lutczyn
ILL/COPY J.Rafal Olbinski
racing sports

6 Netherlands
AD Drukkerij van Wyland BV
AG Ton van Lemmen
ILL John Ruis
COPY Fred Jelsma
printers

7 Hungary .
AD Budavox Telecommunications Foreign
Trading Co Ltd
AG Publishing House of the Art Foundation
DIR Sophia Zupan
DES Ferenc Veszely
ILL Istvan Vidovics
telecommunications

4

5

7

6

Greetings cards
Calendars
Cartes de voeux
Calendriers
Glückwunschkarten
Kalender

1 Belgium
AD de Schutter NV
AG Photogravure de Schutter NV
ILL Hergé

2a-b Italy
AD Litho Gamas
DES/ILL Roberto Glussoni
printers

3 Israel
AD Yaniv Enterprizes Ltd
AG A. Kalderon
DIR/DES A. Kalderon

4 Hungary
AD Publishing House of Books for Youth
ILL Laszló Réber
children's publishing house

5 Switzerland
AD Pierre Bataillard
DES Pierre Bataillard

6a-b Great Britain
AD B.L. Cars Ltd
AG Derek Forsyth Partnership
DIR/DES Michael Staniford
PHOTO Heini Schneebeli
COPY Dana Gibbs
BL cars, voitures BL

7 India
AD Air-India
AG Air-India Art Studio
DES S.N. Surti/S.S. Dabholkar
calendar with ancient playing cards

1

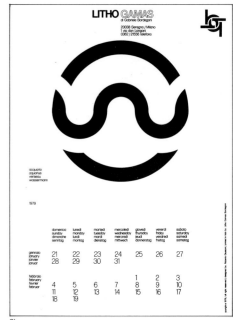

2a

2b

3

4

5

8 United States
AD Smith Kline & French Labs.
DIR A. Neal Siegel
DES Jim Lakis
COPY Gerry Henwood
Ancef post card calendar, calendrier pour les
cartes postales Ancef

9 Great Britain
AD BTR Group of Companies
DES/PHOTO Sam Haskins
calendar for industrial group

6a

6b

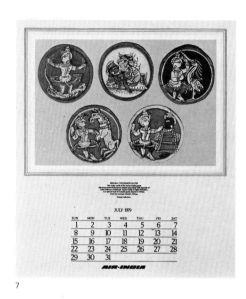

7

8

9

Greetings cards
Calendars
Cartes de voeux
Calendriers
Glückwunschkarten
Kalender

1 Japan
AD Shin-Shirazuna Electric Corporation
AG Media Co Ltd
DIR Hirofumi Suehiro
DES Masakazu Tanabe
PHOTO Sachiko Kuru
calendar

2 Germany
AD BASF Farben & Fasern AG
Unternehmensbereich K & E Druckfarben
DES Friedel Maischen
ILL Gerding & Reiss
K & E Druckfarben
printing inks

3 Germany
AD Voko-Franz Vogt & Co
office furniture calendar,

4 Great Britain
AD Mintex Ltd
AG Frederick Forsyth & Partners
DES Michael Staniford
ILL Barry Lategan

5a-b Great Britain
AD Pentax Ltd
DIR Sam Haskins/Mitsuo Katsui
DES Mitsuo Katsui
PHOTO Sam Haskins
Pentax cameras, appareils de photo Pentax

6 Japan
AD Toyo Ink Inc
AG Ikko Tanaka Design Studio
DIR/DES Ikko Tanaka
inks

1

2

3

4

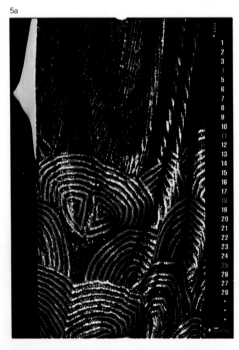

5a

5b

7 Yugoslavia
AD Hidroelektra
DIR Zivko Cule
DES Tomislav Stambuk and Zivko Cule
ILL Nenad Gattin
construction company, compagnie de
construction, Baugesellschaft

8 Germany
AD Volkswagenwerk AG
AG Alpha-G Phototeam
DIR J. Albrecht Cropp
ILL J. Albrecht Cropp
cars, autos

9 Brazil
AD Volkswagen do Brasil SA
AG Alcantara Machado, Periscinoto
Communicaçoes Ltda
DIR Joaquim Gonçalves de Oliveira
ILL Erevan Maizza Chakarian
COPY Enio Basilio Rodrigues
Volkswagen campaign (calendar)

10 United States
AD Mead Paper Corporation
AG Harrison Associates
DIR Peter Harrison
DES Randee Rafkin-Rubin
paper

6

7

8

9

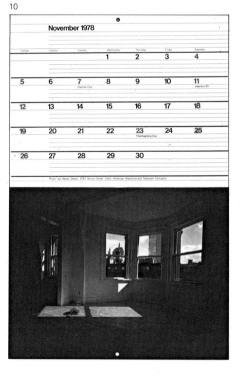

10

Greetings cards
Calendars
Cartes de voeux
Calendriers
Glückwunschkarten
Kalender

1 Great Britain
AD Bloy Eldridge
DES Robert Custance
Christmas card, carte de Noël

2 Great Britain
AD The Small Back Room
DIR/DES Mark Osborne, John Rushton
ILL Helen Cowcher
Christmas card

3 Canada
AD Gingko Design Ltd
AG Harry Agensky Design
DIR/DES Harry Agensky
Christmas card, carte de Noël

4 Brazil
AD Paulo Giovanni Publicidade
DIR Luiz Carlos Pereira Dacunha
DES Carlos Alberto Salles
Christmas card, carte de Noël

5 United States
AD The Robbins Company
AG/DIR/DES Charles Goslin
Christmas card, carte de Noël

6 Great Britain
AD Mike Conrad & Associates
DIR Mike Conrad
Christmas card with token gift, carte de Noël
bon cadeau

7 Great Britain
AD Negus & Negus
DIR/DES Richard Negus
Christmas Card

8 Great Britain
AD Bill Sands
DES Colin Sands
birth announcement,

9 Great Britain
AD Cato Johnson Ltd
DIR/DES/ILL Richard Tilley
Christmas card, carte de Noël

1

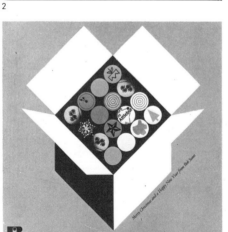

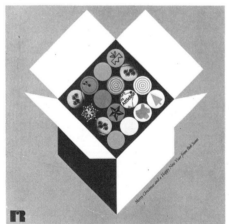

3

6

4   5

7

8

10 Great Britain
AD Brewer Smith and Brewer Maxwell
AG The Small Back Room
DIR/DES Mark Osborne
ILL Tony Donaghue/Helen Cowcher
Christmas card, carte de Noël

11 Great Britain
AD Marisa Martin
DES Richard Ward
Christmas card, carte de Noël

12 Holland
AD Fam. Mlinar
DIR/DES Eduard Mlinar
birth announcement, jouie-part de naissance

13 Great Britain
AD Trickett Associates
AG Trickett & Webb Ltd
DIR/DES Lynn Trickett/Brian Webb
ILL Colin Eusden
Christmas card

14 United States
AD Studio Three D
DIR/DES Stan Baker
New Year's card, carte pour le Nouvel An

15 Great Britain
AD/AG Your Company by Design Ltd
DIR Derrick Holmes
DES Elizabeth Neate
New Years card

16 United States
AD Ruth & Stan Brod
AG Lipson-Jacob Assoc.
DIR/DES Stan Brod
Jewish New Year, Nouvel An Juij

We wish you a very Colourful Christmas, Cato Johnson GLH

9

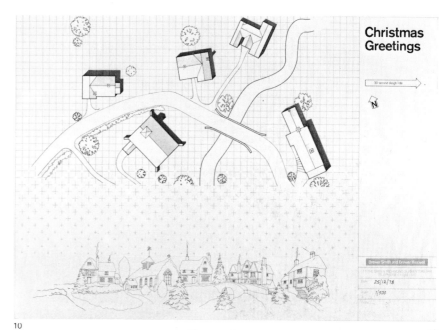

Christmas Greetings

10

12

11

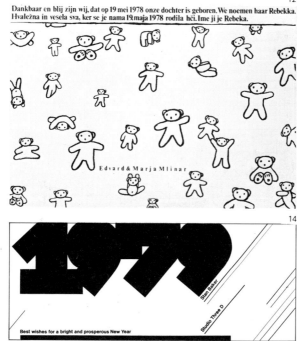

Dankbaar en blij zijn wij, dat op 19 mei 1978 onze dochter is geboren. We noemen haar Rebekka.
Hvaležna in vesela sva, ker se je nama 19.maja 1978 rodila hči. Ime ji je Rebeka.

Edvard & Marja Mlinar

14

Best wishes for a bright and prosperous New Year

13

WE WISH YOU A MERRY CHRISTMAS
TRICKETT ASSOCIATES

15

DAVID LIM
Number 5 -778 Gilford Street
Vancouver B.C. V6G 2N4
682-4043

Personal Greeting Account   No. _____

_____ 19 ___

PAY TO THE
ORDER OF _____ g _____
ONE CHRISTMAS GREETING   GREETINGS

16

Greetings cards
Calendars
Cartes de voeux
Calendriers
Glückwunschkarten
Kalender

1 Great Britain
AD Tullis Russell & Co Ltd
AG Cato Johnson Ltd
DIR/DES/ILL Richard Tilley
advent calendar, calendrier d'Avent

2a-b Great Britain
AD Framemaker Products Ltd
AG John Marsh Design
DIR/DES John Marsh
Christmas card, carte de Noël

3 Holland
AD Anatec BU
AG Integral Design Unit
DES Robert Schaap
New Year's card, carte du Nouvel An

4 Italy
AD Pirelli
AG Centro
DIR/DES Giuseppe De Liso
PHOTO Photo Professional

5 Brazil
AD Volkswagen do Brasil SA
AG Alcantara Machado, Periscinoto
Communicaçaes, Ltd
DIR Deilon Gomes de Lima
PHOTO Eduardo Ribeiro
Christmas card, carte de Noël

6 Japan
AD Otani Memorial Art Museum
DES Laszló Réber
Greetings card, carte de voeux

1

2a

2b

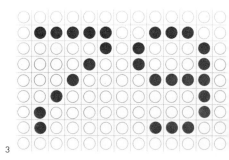

3

4   5

Festeje o Natal à sua maneira, mas festeje com amor.

6